STACK THE DECK!
Crazy Quilts in 4 Easy Steps

Karla Alexander

Martingale™
& COMPANY

CREDITS

President . . . . Nancy J. Martin
CEO . . . . Daniel J. Martin
Publisher . . . . Jane Hamada
Editorial Director. . . . . Mary V. Green
Managing Editor. . . . . Tina Cook
Technical Editor. . . . . Barbara Weiland
Copy Editor . . . . Ellen Balstad
Design Director. . . . . Stan Green
Illustrator. . . . . Laurel Strand
Cover Designer . . . . Stan Green
Text Designer . . . . Jennifer LaRock Shontz
Photographer . . . . Brent Kane

That Patchwork Place® is an imprint of
Martingale & Company™.

Stack the Deck! Crazy Quilts in 4 Easy Steps
© 2002 by Karla Alexander

Martingale & Company
20205 144th Avenue NE
Woodinville, WA 98072-8478 USA
www.martingale-pub.com

Printed in China
07 06 05 04 03   8 7 6 5 4

DEDICATION

This book is dedicated to my three sons, Shane Collins, Kelly Collins, and William Alexander, to whom I will gladly supply quilts–forever. Though my sons are no longer babies, the instinct to wrap each of them in a soft, cuddly quilt continues to this day. Even when my boys are far from me, they will always be close to my heart, especially when wrapped in one of my quilts.

ACKNOWLEDGMENTS

My heartfelt thanks go to:

My husband, Don, for his immeasurable and generous help, encouragement, enthusiasm, and patience while I was writing this crazy book, and for keeping our family in order while I was temporarily "out"! His contribution was enormous.

Sylvia Dorney and the staff at Greenbaum's Quilted Forest for creating an excellent forum for this book, and for their energy, enthusiasm, and help. Special thanks to Lisa Encabo and Joanna Price for their endless offers to help.

Greenbaum's Quilted Forest for generously donating fabric for several of the quilts in this book.

Textile Creations Inc. for supplying a wonderful selection of their beautiful cotton lamé fabric.

> ### MISSION STATEMENT
> We are dedicated to providing quality products and service by working together to inspire creativity and to enrich the lives we touch.

Library of Congress Cataloging-in-Publication Data
Alexander, Karla
    Stack the deck! : crazy quilts in 4 easy steps / Karla Alexander.
       p. cm.
    ISBN 1-56477-434-1
    1. Patchwork–Patterns. 2. Crazy quilts.
3. Rotary cutting. I. Title.
TT835 .A435 2002
746.46' 041–dc21   2002003482

Contents

Introduction

As a young girl, I grew up playing around my mother's sewing machine while she busied herself making clothes for her five kids. With her scraps I sewed Barbie doll clothes. As I got older, I attempted to sew clothing for myself, and in junior high I took the recommended home economics class. The usual clothing assignment remained just that—an assignment without any passion attached.

Then one year my mother gave me a quilt for Christmas. She lovingly pointed out that the Nine Patch blocks were made with pieces from dresses she wore as a young girl as well as pieces from her sister's dresses and her brother's shirts. The blocks, surrounded by a red plaid border, were followed by another row of Nine Patch blocks. In this second round of blocks, I recognized pieces from my old play clothes and from those of my sisters and brothers too.

This simple quilt, with its timeworn hand- and machine-pieced blocks, fascinated me then and continues to inspire me to this day as I stitch new quilts from new fabrics, using the latest in techniques and equipment. I owe a debt of gratitude to my mother for introducing me to quilting—and one to my father too.

In the heart of the Pacific Northwest, beautiful rolling hills are carpeted with every color of green imaginable. While living in Eugene, Oregon, my father would periodically annoy me when driving me somewhere by pulling over to the edge of the roadside and stopping abruptly. "What are you doing?" I would ask impatiently, and, without shifting his gaze from the hillsides, he would say, "Man—how many different colors of green can you see out there?"

Today, I find myself cruising down quilt-shop aisles, gazing at all the tones, tints, and values that are available in quilting fabrics. Like my father, I pull over abruptly, remembering his words and the "Crazy quilt" of greens that covered the hillsides of which he was so fond. I'm sure Dad's annoying driving habit had some influence on my current passion for Crazy quilts—a passion that I share with you in the Crazy quilts and projects in this book.

I have always been fascinated with Crazy quilts, the irregularly pieced and ornately embellished fabric throws that were all the rage during the Victorian era. Those handmade heirlooms represent hours of handwork, something that I don't have time for in my busy life today.

My search for an easier, faster method of making a multipatch quilt that would reflect my passion for the old Crazy quilts led to the technique I share in this book. This technique adds to an idea that I heard vaguely described by a shop customer when I lived in Alaska. I experimented with, and expanded on, the basic idea, and developed a process that simplifies the construction of a Crazy quilt into a block format. The process is easier and less time-consuming than the original method, and you create the blocks for a Crazy quilt by machine in four easy steps.

1. **Stack** large squares of assorted fabrics into a deck, like playing cards.

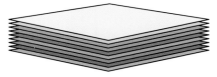

Stack the required number of fabric squares.

2. **Slice** the deck into crazy shapes, following a block cutting and sewing guide for the quilt project you've chosen.

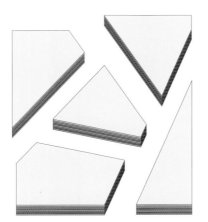

Slice the deck into segments.

3. **Shuffle** the pieces in each stack. (See directions on page 10 for a complete description of how to do this.)

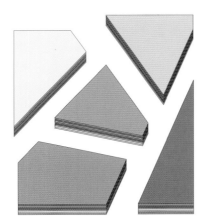

4. **Sew** the pieces in each layer of the deck together to make Crazy blocks—squares that are each made of different fabrics. Trim the resulting blocks to the required size.

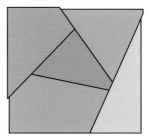

Sew the pieces together.

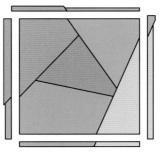

Trim the block to the required size.

It's fun, it's easy, and it's fast. I hope my passion becomes yours as you create your new-century Crazy quilts—with my method. So, let's go a little crazy—together!

—*Karla Alexander*

Getting Started

Before you can begin your first Crazy block project, there are some things to do. First, you'll want to choose a project to determine the number of fabrics you'll need. Then you'll have to go shopping for the fabrics or look for them in your stash. Be sure to read "Choosing Fabrics for Crazy Blocks" below before you select your fabrics.

The project you choose will provide the appropriate block cutting and sewing guide, either for a whole block style or a two-sided block style. Detailed descriptions of these styles are provided in "Choosing a Crazy Block Style" on page 8, along with information you will need—especially if you decide to design your own Crazy block cutting and sewing guides.

CHOOSING FABRICS FOR CRAZY BLOCKS

Crazy quilts can be made from a wide assortment of colors and prints, just like any traditionally pieced scrap quilt. They can also be more controlled, with a planned color scheme or theme-related fabrics such as holiday or baby prints. For example, making a quilt entirely out of blue and yellow prints or an assortment of pastel flannels creates a perfect baby quilt.

You will need from six to twenty-four fabrics for the Crazy quilt patterns in this book. For an even scrappier look, you can choose more fabrics than the number specified in the directions for the quilt you are making. However, until you've tried this method with one of the simpler projects, I recommend that you begin with no more than

the required number of fabrics indicated in the project directions.

The directions for each project include a block cutting and sewing guide, which is similar to a template. Each guide is divided into four or more segments. *To meet the minimum fabric-square requirement for this block-piecing method,* you will need to stack the *same* number of fabric squares in each required deck as there are segments in the block guide. For example, if there are four segments in the guide, you will need a *minimum* of four different fabric squares for the blocks; if there are six segments, you'll need at least six different fabric squares; and so on. However, I recommend starting with no fewer than six fabrics—*even if you are following a block cutting and sewing guide with only four segments*—so the blocks are scrappier; for the projects in this book, you will start with no fewer than six fabrics. Using more fabrics means you will sometimes make an extra block or two. This is good because it makes it easier to come up with a pleasing block arrangement for your quilt top. Your blocks will be scrappier because you have more fabrics moving positions. For example, if you have four segments and six fabrics, two fabrics in the total assortment will not appear in each finished block. Each block will feature a different combination of only four of the six fabrics.

Illustrated on page 7 (top left) is an example of what happens when the number of different fabrics and the number of block segments are equal. In this case, only four different fabrics were used to make the nine four-segment blocks. Every block is a combination of the same four fabrics, with the fabrics moving from position to position in numerical order within the individual blocks. Some blocks are exactly alike.

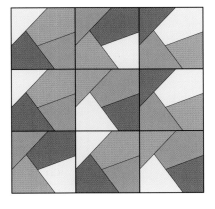

Below is an example of what happens when the number of different fabrics used is greater than the number of block segments. In this case, nine different fabrics were used in a deck to make the four-segment blocks. Study the position of segment 1 in each block and you will see that each block has a different combination of colors. I think you'll agree that the second quilt illustrated is far more interesting than the one above because there are nine different fabrics moving through the blocks.

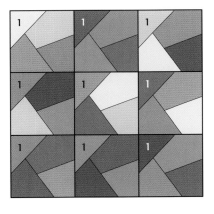

At right is another visual example of how one color shifts or rotates through the blocks. With this six-segment block, a new color or fabric is always introduced in the segment 1 position. The fabric moves in numerical order through the remaining positions and is last seen in the segment 6 position. Every time you introduce a new fabric into a block,

you are creating a new arrangement of fabrics so no two blocks from a deck look the same.

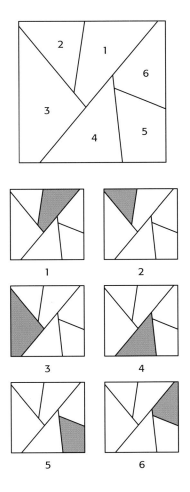

Note: If you use more fabrics than the number of block segments, such as nine fabrics to make nine six-segment blocks, the extra three fabrics will not show up in every block. For example, the fabric you start with—fabric 1—will appear only in the first six blocks that you make. Using more fabrics than segments results in more blocks that are different from each other.

If you *still* have questions about how this technique works, just follow the instructions for stacking and slicing a deck (see pages 9–10) and use two or three more fabrics than the number of segments in the block you've chosen. It's good practice before you start your first project—and doing and seeing are believing and understanding!

CHOOSING A CRAZY BLOCK STYLE

I use two different block styles to make Crazy blocks—the whole block style and the two-sided block style.

Whole Block: This block style may have as few as three segments or as many as seven. With this style, you stack and slice the deck, and shuffle the fabric segments in the order shown, following the **red** numbers. Then you follow the **blue** numbers to sew the segments back together to make each block. *Note that the sewing order is the exact reverse of the cutting order for a whole block, no matter how many segments there are.* Blocks made in this style are best when they have an *odd* number of segments.

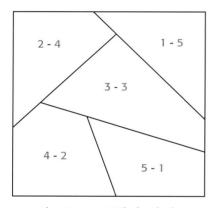

**Five-Segment Whole Block
Cutting and Sewing Guide**
The red number in each segment
indicates the cutting order;
the blue number indicates
the sewing order.

Two-Sided Block: This block style has a left side and a right side. The deck of squares is cut into somewhat equal halves first. Then each half is cut into two or more segments. The letters *L* and *R* in the cutting and sewing guides for these blocks refer to the left and right halves or sides of the block. After the decks are stacked, sliced, and shuffled, the pieces in each half are joined. The resulting pieces (half-blocks) are trimmed as needed (see page 14). Then they are sewn together to complete the blocks. Finally they are trimmed one more time

to the correct block size for the project. This style is best for blocks designed with an *even* number of segments.

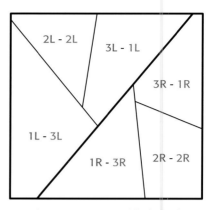

**Six-Segment Two-Sided Block
Cutting and Sewing Guide**
The red number in each segment
indicates the cutting order;
the blue number indicates
the sewing order.

Note: The block cutting and sewing guide for each project includes the required cut size for the fabric squares. However, you can use these cutting guides to cut larger or smaller squares for other Crazy quilt projects that you design after you try my methods. And, you can come up with cutting variations of your own. The sky's the limit!

Almost any combination of segments will work for a Crazy block. For example, on small blocks, or on fabric that is challenging to sew, such as velvet, I often choose a block style with only a few segments, such as three or four, because they are easier and quicker to sew. Cutting more segments means more sewing—it's just that simple.

If you're like me, it won't take long to get hooked on these Crazy quilts, and then you'll find that using more fabrics equals more fun (and a good reason to visit your favorite quilt shop!). The great thing about my Crazy-quilt technique is that you can use up leftovers from other projects, start with brand new fabrics, or use a combination of both to create blocks.

Making the Crazy Blocks

Are you ready for some fun and easy quiltmaking? The projects in this book are simple to cut and sew; they're just a little crazy, but that's all! Follow the directions below to make your blocks; then refer to "Quiltmaking Techniques" beginning on page 15 for information on how to assemble and finish your Crazy quilt.

STACKING THE DECK

Once you've decided which project you want to make, select your fabrics, keeping the style of the fabric and the colors in mind. If you begin with fabrics that are jarring and don't mix well together, your Crazy quilt will be even more jarring. To keep things under control, I use the 10-foot rule, which my students find helpful too. Try it as you select your fabrics and I'm sure you'll find it easy to choose great fabric combinations for your quilts.

After you've selected the fabrics you want to use, it's time to cut and stack the squares. Refer to the specific cutting directions for the project you chose. As you stack the squares, alternate dark, medium, and light values in each deck. Make sure you do not have duplicate squares of any one fabric in any one deck. Also keep in mind that the top fabric in the deck will eventually be shuffled to the bottom of the deck, so make sure there is contrast between the top and bottom fabrics.

For example, if you have three light-value squares in your deck, don't stack them directly on top of one another. Instead, alternate them between squares of medium and dark values. Of course, you are making a Crazy quilt and eventually some fabrics may end up side by side somewhere in the quilt, but you can keep the blending to a minimum by stacking your cutting decks as described above.

THE 10-FOOT RULE

Stack your selected bolts of fabric—one on top of another—on a counter; or stand bolts side by side. Then back up approximately 10 feet and take a look. Do the fabrics harmonize with one another? Does one fabric jump out from the rest? If so, that fabric may need a similar companion. For example, if you have just one red fabric in the mix and your eye goes right to it every time you look at the stack, try adding another red (or two) to the mix for a better balance. On the other hand, if you have three fabrics from the same color group, use the 10-foot rule to determine if they appear to blend together too much—and look like one piece of fabric. For example, if you've chosen three medium blue fabrics and they seem muddled

from 10 feet away, replace at least one of them with a brighter blue, a blue that has another color in the print, or something else that will liven up the fabric grouping. Pep up the color mix. Three grass greens won't be very exciting, but if you replace one with lime, chartreuse, or sage, you're bound to have a more interesting block.

One of my favorite tools for evaluating a fabric mix is a simple door peephole, available at any home improvement center. Looking through a door peephole distances you from your choices and helps you determine if you have a "jumper"—a fabric that jumps out at you—or if there are too many fabrics that just blend into each other, creating a muddy look.

SLICING THE DECK

When your decks are stacked and ready to cut, you have two cutting options; choose the one that is most comfortable for your sewing style.

▸ Cut with a paper template. Make the template by following the specific block cutting and sewing guide provided with the project directions. You will need the same number of paper templates as there are required decks of fabric for your project.

▸ Cut free-form, referring to the block cutting and sewing guide with the project directions.

To cut with a template:

1. In the project directions, refer to the block cutting and sewing guide for the cut size of the squares. Draw a square of this size on a piece of clean newsprint paper, freezer paper, or the unprinted side of wrapping paper. Then refer to the guide to draw the cutting lines. When drawing the lines, it's not critical to have the measurements for the segments; just trust your eyes. When you're satisfied with your template, make as many copies of it as there are fabric decks required for your quilt.

2. Cut the template(s) out around the outer edges of the square(s).

3. Pin a paper template to the top of a stacked fabric deck. Pin through each numbered segment in the template to secure the pieces. Flat flower-head pins work great for this task because you'll be placing your acrylic ruler on top of the template when cutting and the ruler won't "rock" as it would if you used pins with round heads.

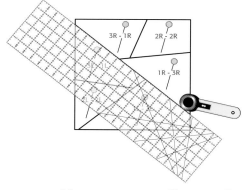

4. Use your rotary cutter with your ruler to slice through the paper template and all layers of fabric on every solid line. Be sure to make the cuts in numerical order, following the red numbers on the block segments in the guide.

5. Remove the pins and the paper template pieces. Reassemble the template pieces to one side of the work surface to use as a reference. Now you're ready to "shuffle the deck" as described below.

To cut free-form:

Refer to the block cutting and sewing guide for the project you are making and cut the decks free-hand. If you think you need a guide on the fabric, you can use a chalk marker to draw the cutting lines on the top layer of the decks. When you use this method, don't worry about cutting every deck the same way. Every finished block you make will be slightly different—and all the "crazier"!

1. Lay your rotary cutting ruler on top of the stacked fabrics and make the first cut as indicated in the block cutting and sewing guide. Keeping the deck together, shift the ruler to make the next cut.

2. Continue cutting the deck into segments, referring to the block guide. Now you're ready to "shuffle the deck" as described below.

SHUFFLING THE DECK

Shuffling the deck is always the same process, regardless of how many layers or segments there are or the block style (whole or two-sided) you've chosen. And, no matter how many segments you cut, *you shuffle each deck only once.* Refer to the illustration of how to shuffle a five-segment whole block on page 11 as you study the following directions for shuffling the deck.

Working with one numbered segment stack at a time:

1. Remove the top layer of the segment 1 stack and place it on the bottom of the stack.

2. Remove the top 2 layers from the segment 2 stack and place them on the bottom of the stack.

3. Remove the top 3 layers from the segment 3 stack and place them on the bottom of the stack.

4. Continue shuffling each segment stack in numerical order in the same manner as steps 1–3. Remove from the top and reposition to the bottom *the same number of fabrics as the number of the segment stack you are shuffling,* until all but the last segment stack have been shuffled.

5. As you complete the shuffle of each deck, arrange the segment stacks on a piece of paper and pin in place. Then trace around the segment shapes with a pencil to draw a template reference for the deck. Keep the segment stacks pinned to the paper until you are ready to sew.

6. To determine where to begin sewing first, refer to the specific project or number the segment stacks in the opposite order from the cutting order. For example, the last two segments cut should be numbered 1 and 2. The segment cut before that will be 3, the one before that will be 4, and so on. The very first segment cut will be the last and highest number. Once you have determined the sewing order, use a pencil and note the number on the template reference made in step 5, underneath the appropriate segment.

SEWING THE BLOCKS

It's important to keep the segment stacks in their shuffled order while sewing; otherwise you'll end up duplicating a fabric within a block. For example, after chain sewing all layers of the segment 1 and segment 2 stacks together, the first layer always needs to be returned to the top of the stack, followed by the second layer, and so on. It's easy to reverse the order while ironing or clipping the segments apart, so I secure a safety pin in the top layer of the segment 1 stack as a reminder. When you begin sewing again, you'll automati-cally know the combined segments are in the right sequence if the safety pin is on top of the stack. If the pin is on the bottom of the stack, you probably reversed the order and you will need to correct it before continuing. Keep the safety pin in place until *all* the blocks have been sewn.

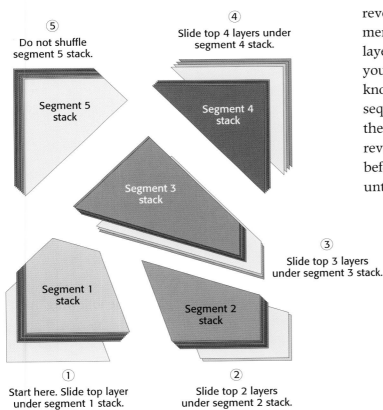

⑤
Do not shuffle
segment 5 stack.

Segment 5 stack

④
Slide top 4 layers under segment 4 stack.

Segment 4 stack

Segment 3 stack

③
Slide top 3 layers under segment 3 stack.

Segment 1 stack

Segment 2 stack

①
Start here. Slide top layer under segment 1 stack.

②
Slide top 2 layers under segment 2 stack.

Sewing Whole Blocks

1. Unpin the segment 1 and 2 stacks and peel off the top pieces from each. Flip segment 2 onto segment 1 with right sides facing, and stitch the pieces together.

2. Pick up the next layer from the segment 1 and 2 stacks and sew them together in the same manner as step 1. You can chain sew the units together as shown below, continuing until all the segment 1 and segment 2 pieces are stitched together in pairs. The fabric color of each piece in position 1 should be different.

4. With right sides together, sew segment 3 on top of the 1-2 units you just made as shown below. Again, you can chain stitch the units.

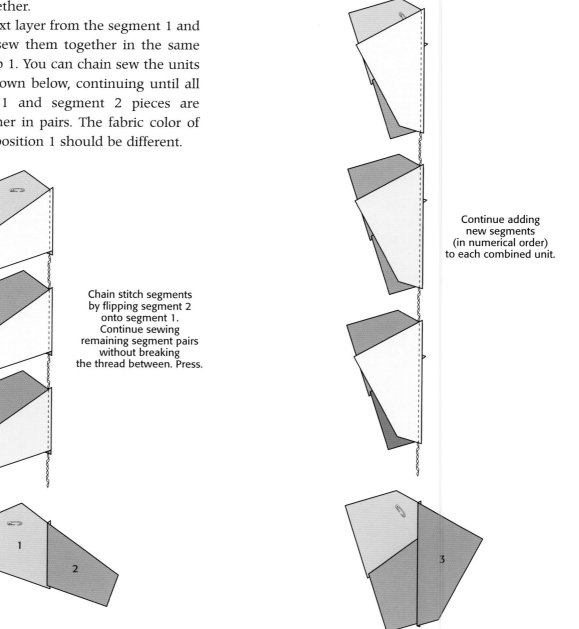

Chain stitch segments by flipping segment 2 onto segment 1. Continue sewing remaining segment pairs without breaking the thread between. Press.

Continue adding new segments (in numerical order) to each combined unit.

3. Press the 1-2 units open. Then clip them apart and restack them in their original order.

5. Press the units open, clip them apart, and stack them in their original order. Continue adding segments in numerical order until all the segments are sewn into blocks.

SEWING TWO-SIDED BLOCKS

Sewing two-sided blocks is similar to sewing whole blocks, but each half of the block is pieced first and then the two halves (left side and right side) are sewn together. Study the sample piecing illustrations to understand the shuffling and sewing process.

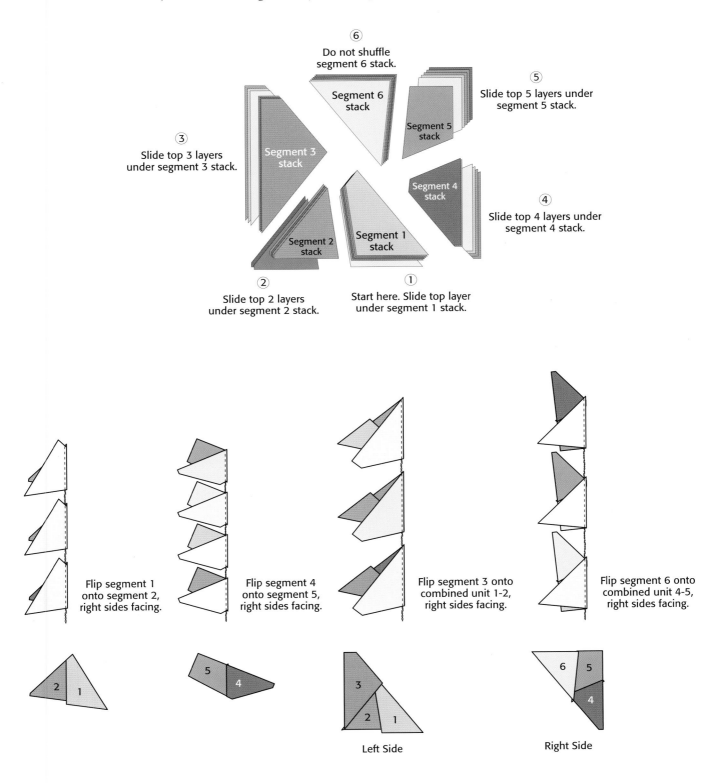

Left Side

Right Side

Note: Before you can sew the two halves of the block together, you must trim away the uneven edges so you can sew a perfect ¼"-wide seam. You only need to trim off a sliver, just enough to make a straight edge.

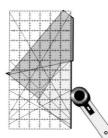

Sliver-trim inside edges of both right and left halves of the block.

To complete each two-sided block:

1. Carefully align the 2 sides or halves of the block so that when stitched together they will roughly create a square. That means that the outer edges of the block may not align when you are sewing, but when you open up the block, it will more or less be a square rather than a rectangle. Press the seam allowance in either direction.

2. Lay a square rotary-cutting ruler on top of the finished blocks and trim to the size specified in the pattern instructions.

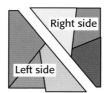

Align left and right sides to create a square rather than a rectangle.

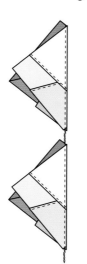

Flip and sew the right side onto the left side. Continue to chain stitch the remaining sides or halves together.

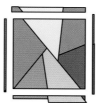

Square up blocks to size indicated in pattern.

DESIGNING YOUR OWN CRAZY QUILT

You can design a quilt of any size. Choose a block size, arrange the block layout, and cut the squares. As you plan your quilt, remember the following things:

- One fabric square (any size) represents one finished block.

- After piecing and squaring up, the finished block size will be approximately 2" to 2½" smaller than the original cut size of the squares you cut for the blocks.

- You will need the same number of fabric squares as the number of blocks you need for your desired quilt layout. For example, if your quilt layout is five blocks across and seven down, you will need a total of thirty-five squares of fabric to begin the block piecing process.

- Use a variety of contrasting colors and textures—the more the "crazier."

One fabric square represents one finished block.

- To determine how many blocks you need for a bed quilt, refer to the chart below.

STANDARD MATTRESS SIZES	
Crib:	23" x 46"
Twin:	39" x 75"
Double:	54" x 75"
Queen:	60" x 80"
King:	76" x 80"

Quiltmaking Techniques

 A sewing machine in good working order, good-quality supplies and tools, stitching accuracy, and a whole lot of passion go into my recipe for a successful and enjoyable quilting experience. The following tools and supplies will make your Crazy-quilt experience fun and easy.

TOOLS AND SUPPLIES

Rotary cutter. Choose a medium to large rotary cutter. The blade must be sharp—you will be cutting through several layers of fabric at once to create your Crazy patches.

Rotary cutting mat. I suggest one that is 17" x 23".

Acrylic rulers. A 6" x 24" ruler is great for cutting fabric into strips. Depending on your project, a 6" x 6" or a 12½" x 12½" square ruler is essential for cutting squares and trimming pieced blocks.

Sewing thread. I recommend good-quality, 100 percent–cotton thread for piecing. Match the thread to the general value of the fabrics. In most cases you can use light, medium, and dark values of tan and gray thread to simplify thread selection.

Quilting thread. Choosing the quilting thread for your finished quilt top is usually the last decision to make. It is also one of my favorite steps. Depending on the project, I use silky rayon, 100 percent cotton, or metallic thread. Always buy the best you can afford.

Silk pins or flat flower-head pins. For most projects in this book, you will pin a template to the fabric stack. Your ruler will lie flat on top of the template if using fine silk pins or flat flower-head pins. Avoid round-headed pins—they cause the ruler to rock on top of the pinned fabric stack, resulting in inaccurate cutting.

Bodkin. Thread elastic or cord through a casing with a bodkin, which is shaped like a long, blunt needle. Some bodkins work like tweezers, grasping and holding the elastic securely. A strong safety pin can substitute for a bodkin, but it may pop open inside the casing.

Seam ripper. Keep a seam ripper handy—you might need one for easy stitch removal.

Sewing machine. Make sure your machine is in good working order and adjust the tensions for a balanced straight stitch. Depending on the style of machine quilting you prefer, you will need either a walking foot or a darning foot.

ASSEMBLING THE QUILT TOP

Follow the quilt assembly directions for each quilt project. With some patterns, you'll have extra blocks to rotate in and out as you arrange and rearrange the blocks to your liking. When the project is complete, use any leftover blocks to make a coordinating pillow, or attach a label to an extra block and sew it to the back of your quilt.

ADDING THE BORDERS

1. Refer to the cutting chart for each individual project and cut the required number of border strips for your quilt.

2. Remove selvages and sew the border strips together to make one long piece. Press the seams open.

3. Arrange the quilt top on a large flat surface and measure the length through the vertical center. Cut two side border strips to that measurement.

4. Fold the quilt top in half crosswise to find and mark the centers. Repeat with the side border strips.

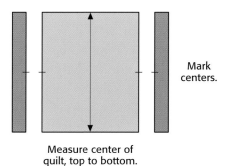

Mark centers.

Measure center of quilt, top to bottom.

5. With centers and ends matching, pin and sew the border strips to the side edges of the quilt top, easing in any excess as needed (the side edges of the quilt top may not be exactly the same length as the center where you took the measurement).

6. Press the seams toward the border strips unless directed otherwise in the individual project instructions.

7. Repeat steps 4–6 to add the top and bottom border strips.

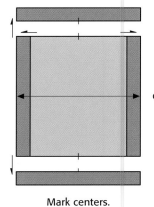

Measure center of quilt, side to side, including borders.

Mark centers.

8. Repeat steps 1–7 for any additional borders.

ADDING APPLIQUÉS

Some of the projects included in this book have appliqués that were applied with fusible web. Transfer-paper-backed fusible web is available in lightweight and heavyweight versions. I used the lightweight version and then embellished the raw edges with machine buttonhole stitching, straight stitching, zigzagging, or satin stitching. If you do not plan to add stitching, choose a heavyweight fusible web for best results.

1. Trace each part of the selected appliqué design onto the paper side of the fusible web. Your design will be the mirror image of the provided pattern, but when finished will be the same image as the finished appliqué in the quilt.

2. Cut out the traced designs, leaving at least a ¼" margin around each one.

Fusible Appliqué Shape

3. Position each fusible shape on the wrong side of the desired fabric and press to attach to the fabric, following the manufacturer's directions. Cut out each shape, following the traced lines on the fusible web.

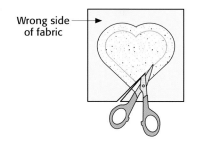

Wrong side of fabric

4. Arrange shapes in position on the quilt top and fuse in place following the manufacturer's directions.

5. Stitch around the raw edges of each appliqué shape with a stitch of your choice—zigzag, satin, straight, or buttonhole stitches are recommended.

EMBELLISHING YOUR QUILT

After you've created your blocks and assembled your project, you can use basic machine or hand embroidery to jazz up your blocks as desired. Just for fun, I used a little machine embroidery on "Velvet Pillow" shown on page 71 as a seam embellishment. Hand embroidery is also a nice choice. For your projects, use embroidery floss or silk ribbon and try some of the stitches shown at right.

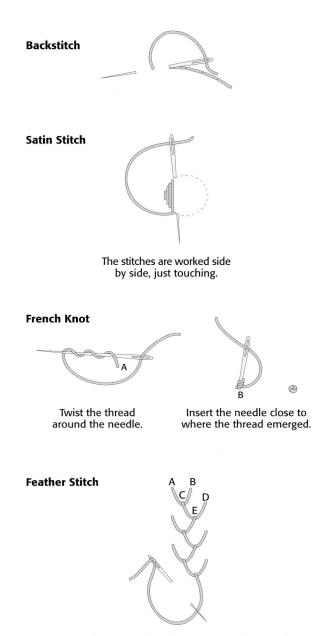

Backstitch

Satin Stitch

The stitches are worked side by side, just touching.

French Knot

Twist the thread around the needle.

Insert the needle close to where the thread emerged.

Feather Stitch

Bring the needle up at A, then down at B, forming a U shape. Bring the needle back up at C to form the "catch," then down at D, once again forming a U shape.

Layering and Basting the Quilt Sandwich

1. Prepare the backing, following the cutting chart for the chosen project.
2. Lay the backing out, wrong side up, on a large, flat surface. Use masking tape to hold it in place, making sure it is smooth and free of wrinkles, and take care not to stretch it. If layering the quilt on your carpet is the only option, you can use T-pins instead of masking tape to attach it to the carpet.
3. Smooth the batting into place on top of the backing, removing any wrinkles. The backing should be 2" to 3" larger all around than the batting.
4. Center the pieced top, right side up, on the batting. Make sure that the quilt top is "square" with the backing.
5. Choose one of the following methods to baste the quilt layers together to prepare for quilting. The first two are the most common; the third is my favorite.

Hand Basting

1. With a large needle and long thread, baste the layers together. Begin in the center of the quilt and baste diagonally with large stitches to each corner.
2. Baste a grid of horizontal and vertical rows, spacing them approximately 6" apart. Finish with a basting stitch around all 4 edges.
3. Quilt as desired by hand or machine.

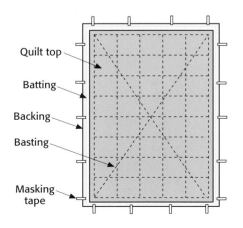

Pin Basting

1. Using 1" safety pins, pin the layers together. Working from the center out, space the pins 5" to 6" apart across the surface.

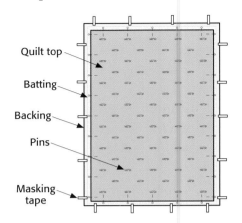

2. Quilt as desired by hand or machine, removing pins that are in the way of your stitching pattern.

Spray Basting

I love to spray baste my quilt layers together. This speedy method works especially well when using cotton or cotton-blend battings. I use 505 Spray and Fix, a temporary fabric adhesive that doesn't leave any residue or gum up the needle. It dissipates as soon as it is washed or fluffed in the dryer. Be sure to work in a well-ventilated area if you decide to try this method.

1. Arrange the quilt layers as described in "Layering and Basting the Quilt Sandwich" at left, but lay a large sheet on the work surface first. This underlayer will catch any overspray.

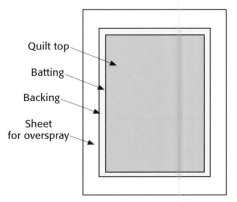

Make sure the sheet is smooth, wrinkle free, and securely attached to the work surface before you add and secure the quilt layers.

Note: I keep a large, old sheet on hand to protect my work surface when spray basting. I wash the sheet in cool water and dry it in the dryer after each use.

2. Fold back the upper quarter of the quilt top on itself, and then fold again so you have exposed the upper half of the batting.
3. Fold the batting in the same manner to expose the upper half of the backing.

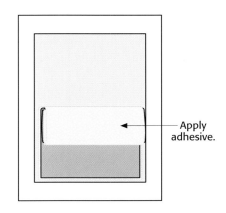

4. Using the fabric spray adhesive, lightly spray the lower half of the exposed section of the batting. Gently replace it on the backing.
5. Apply adhesive to the remainder of the exposed batting and relace it on the backing.
6. Use the side of the spray can as a tool and slide it over the replaced batting section to smooth out any wrinkles.

7. Now spray the exposed batting again and smooth the quilt top in place on top. *Spray the batting, not the quilt top.* You're half done!

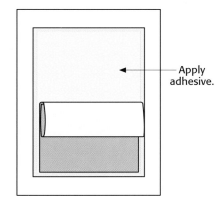

8. Repeat steps 3–8 with the remaining half of the quilt layers to complete the basting process.

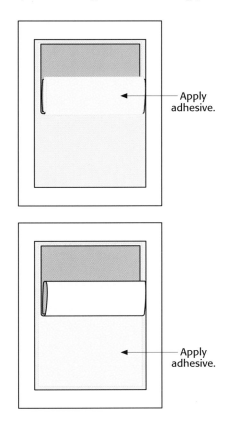

9. Remove masking tape or T-pins and turn the quilt over. Carefully smooth out any wrinkles.

10. Quilt as desired by hand or machine.

Note: After quilting and binding my quilt, I like to tumble it in a warm dryer with a damp washcloth for about fifteen minutes. This helps the adhesive dissipate more quickly—without actually washing the new quilt.

BINDING YOUR QUILT

Binding finishes the raw edges of your quilt. My preference is double-fold, straight-grain binding. Select one of the prints you used in your quilt or introduce a new print for the binding. I often use busy prints in my quilts, so for binding I frequently choose a print that appears as a solid from a distance.

1. Trim the batting and backing even with the quilt-top edges.
2. Refer to the cutting chart for the quilt project and cut the required number of binding strips.
3. Remove selvages and join the binding strips right sides together as shown, to make one long piece of binding. Trim excess and press seam allowances open to reduce bulk.

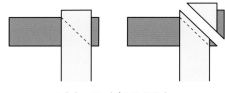

Joining Straight-Cut Strips

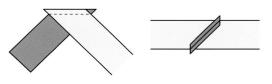

Joining Bias-Cut Strips

4. Fold the binding strip in half lengthwise with wrong sides together and press lightly.
5. Beginning 10" to 18" from one corner, position the binding on the front of the quilt with raw edges aligned. Use a 3/8"-wide seam allowance and a walking foot to sew the binding to the

quilt. Stop stitching 3/8" from the corner and carefully backstitch 2 to 3 stitches. Clip the thread and remove the quilt from the sewing machine.

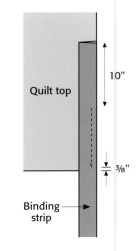

6. Rotate the quilt 90° and fold the binding up; then fold the binding back down, with the fold even with the stitched edge and the raw edges aligned on the next side of the quilt. A little pleat will form at the corner; pin in place to secure for stitching.
7. Begin stitching at the folded edge. Continue stitching to the next corner, then stop, turn 90°, and position the binding for the next side as described in step 6.

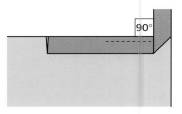

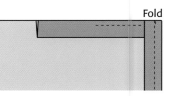

8. When you have reached a point approximately 10" from the starting point, stop and remove the quilt from the sewing machine.

9. To join the binding ends, fold back each end of the binding and arrange so they meet in the center of the unsewn portion of the binding strips. Crease the folded edges by finger-pressing.

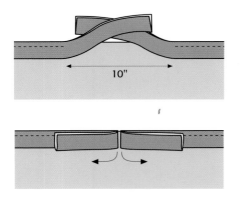

10. Unfold both ends of the binding and match the centers at the pressed fold line of the binding strip, forming an X as shown. Pin and sew the 2 ends together on the finger-pressed fold lines. Trim the excess binding ¼" from the stitching line. Finger-press the seam open, refold, and complete the stitching to attach the binding to the quilt edge.

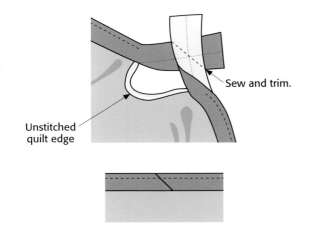

11. Fold the binding over the quilt edges to the backing side. With the folded edge covering the machine stitching, hand sew in place, mitering the corners as you go.

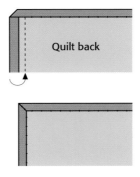

LABELING YOUR QUILT

Finish your quilt by adding a label to the back that includes your name, the name of the quilt, and the quilt completion date. Extra information, such as the name of the recipient if it's a gift, is nice to add. Use a permanent fabric marker to write the information on a piece of fabric and then attach it to the back of your quilt. To make it easier to write on the fabric, apply a piece of freezer paper to the wrong side of the label fabric; press the shiny side of the paper to the fabric with a warm, dry iron. Remove the paper after you've completed the label and before you sew it to the quilt back.

In Full Bloom Quilt

BY KARLA ALEXANDER

This colorful quilt is my interpretation of my mother's home, which is always in full bloom—even in the wintertime.

Note: It's best to make 72 blocks, even though the quilt requires only 59. This gives you more options when arranging the blocks for the quilt top. The leftover blocks are cut into smaller squares to make the coordinating neck roll (page 26) and pillow (page 27), which are a nice bonus.

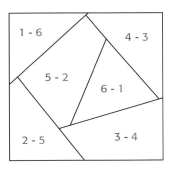

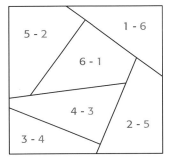

Block Cutting and Sewing Guides
Cut Size: 11" x 11"

FABRIC SELECTION

This quilt and coordinating neck roll and pillow require floral fabrics with an uneven distribution of swirling flower, vine, and branch motifs. Fabrics with a variety of multicolored medium to large floral motifs blend together well in this type of Crazy quilt.

You will need a total of 30 fabrics in a range of values. To get started, choose 5 different floral fabrics: a light, medium-light, medium, medium-dark, and dark. Use the 10-foot rule described on page 9 to determine whether or not your selections give you a subtle gradation of value from light to dark. Adjust your fabric choices if necessary. Repeat this process 5 more times.

Examples of light-value florals

After choosing the fabrics, arrange them by value into 5 groups: A—Light floral; B—Medium-light floral; C—Medium floral; D—Medium-dark floral; and E—Dark floral.

Note: It's always nice to use fabric from your personal stash, so check the fabric requirements before you head for the store. This is a very practical approach to assembling fabrics for value group A because this group requires a small number of squares. You may already have enough light prints in your stash that you can use for this project.

Note: The more fabrics you use in this quilt, the easier it will be to create a blended effect for a truly "blooming" quilt. You can use as many different prints per value group as there are required squares. For example, collect 12 different medium-light florals for group B because the cutting list requires 12 squares, and so on.

MATERIALS FOR CRAZY BLOCKS AND QUILT

Yardage is based on 42"-wide fabric, with 40" of usable width after preshrinking.

⅜ yd. *each* of 6 different light florals (group A) for Crazy blocks

⅜ yd. *each* of 6 different medium-light florals (group B) for Crazy blocks

⅜ yd. *each* of 6 different medium florals (group C) for Crazy blocks

⅜ yd. *each* of 6 different medium-dark florals (group D) for Crazy blocks

⅜ yd. *each* of 6 different dark florals (group E) for Crazy blocks

1⅛ yds. dark floral for setting triangles

⅝ yd. dark floral for binding

3½ yds. fabric for backing

56" x 77" piece of batting

CUTTING FOR CRAZY BLOCKS AND QUILT

All measurements include ¼"-wide seam allowances. Cut all strips across the fabric width (crosswise grain).

From each of the 6 light florals (group A), cut:

1 square, 11" x 11", for a total of 6 squares for Crazy blocks

From each of the 6 medium-light florals (group B), cut:

2 squares, each 11" x 11", for a total of 12 squares for Crazy blocks

From each of the 6 medium florals (group C), cut:

2 squares, each 11" x 11", for a total of 12 squares for Crazy blocks

From each of the 6 medium-dark florals (group D), cut:

3 squares, each 11" x 11", for a total of 18 squares for Crazy blocks

From each of the 6 dark florals (group E), cut:

4 squares, each 11" x 11", for a total of 24 squares for Crazy blocks

From the dark floral for setting triangles, cut:

2 strips, each 13" wide; crosscut strips into 5 squares, each 13" x 13". Cut each square twice diagonally to yield 20 side setting triangles.

1 strip, 9" wide; crosscut strip into 2 squares, each 9" x 9". Cut each square once diagonally to yield 4 corner setting triangles.

From the dark floral for binding, cut:

7 strips, each 2½" x 42"

PIECING THE CRAZY BLOCKS

1. Following the chart below, stack the 11" squares in the required number of decks, with each deck containing *6 different prints of the same fabric group* (A, B, C, D, E). Secure each deck with a pin through all layers until ready to sew.

2. Referring to "Making the Crazy Blocks" on page 9 and using one or both of the six-segment block cutting and sewing guides on page 23, make 72 Crazy blocks. Refer to the chart for the number of Crazy blocks required from each fabric group. Trim the blocks to 8" x 8".

Fabric Group	Number of Decks	Number of Crazy Blocks
A. Light floral	1	6
B. Medium-light floral	2	12
C. Medium floral	2	12
D. Medium-dark floral	3	18
E. Dark floral	4	24

Note: I like to begin piecing with the light floral fabrics and work my way to the darker ones. This allows me to arrange the blocks on my design wall as I go and watch the design flow from light to dark.

ASSEMBLING THE QUILT TOP

1. Arrange 59 Crazy blocks on point, beginning with a vertical row of 3 light-floral blocks in the center and working outward with progressively darker blocks. You should have 13 Crazy blocks left for the pillows (see pages 26 and 27 for assembly directions).

2. Look through a door peephole (see "The 10-Foot Rule" on page 9) to check the blending of colors from one block to another. Move and turn the blocks, until you are satisfied with their arrangement. I try to avoid having identical prints side by side. Remember that you have extra blocks for the pillows, so use those that create the best possible block arrangement for the quilt top. Use the remaining ones for the pillows.

3. Add the dark floral side and corner setting triangles to the quilt layout.
4. Pin and sew the blocks and *side setting triangles* together in diagonal rows. Press the seams in opposite directions from row to row so they will nestle together when you join the rows.
5. Add the corner triangles to complete the quilt top. Press the seams toward the corner triangles.

FINISHING YOUR QUILT

1. Divide the backing fabric into 2 panels, each approximately 63" long, and remove the selvages.
2. Sew the panels together along 2 long edges to make the backing. Press the seam to one side.
3. Layer the quilt top with batting and backing, with the backing seam across the quilt width. Baste the layers together using your favorite method (see page 18).
4. Machine or hand quilt as desired.
5. Trim the quilt batting and backing even with the quilt-top edges and bind the quilt (see page 20).
6. Add a label to the back and enjoy your new quilt!

CUTTING CRAZY BLOCKS FOR GARDEN NECK ROLL AND GARDEN PILLOW

To begin, cut each of the remaining "In Full Bloom" 8"-square Crazy blocks into 4" squares. You will combine these 4" pieced squares with additional 4" fabric squares to make the neck roll and pillow as instructed. Note that all of the group C blocks were used in the quilt top; only blocks from groups A, B, D, and E will be used in the neck roll and pillow.

Fabric Group	Number of 4" Squares
A. Light floral	12
B. Medium-light floral	16
D. Medium-dark floral	8
E. Dark floral	16

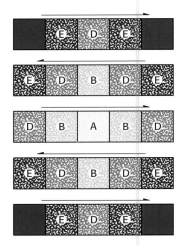

By KARLA ALEXANDER, 6" x 17"
This pillow has lavender sprinkled inside the lining.
The fragrance is said to enhance sleep.

Materials for Garden Neck Roll

Yardage is based on 42"-wide fabric, with 40" of usable width after preshrinking. Refer to "Cutting Crazy Blocks for Garden Neck Roll and Garden Pillow" on page 25 for instructions regarding the floral 4" squares listed below.

1 light floral 4" square for neck roll top
4 medium-light floral 4" squares for neck roll top
8 medium-dark floral 4" squares for neck roll top
8 dark floral 4" squares for neck roll top
⅝ yd. dark floral for corner squares and end cuffs
⅝ yd. muslin for lining
21" x 21" piece of batting
Polyester fiberfill for stuffing
¼ cup dried lavender (optional)
Spray-basting adhesive (optional)
2 yds. of strong cord
2 large buttons, up to 1" diameter (optional)

Cutting for Garden Neck Roll

All measurements include ¼"-wide seam allowances.

From the ⅝ yd. of dark floral, cut:
   1 square, 8" x 8"; crosscut square into 4 corner
      squares, each 4" x 4".
   2 strips, each 4½" x 20½", for end cuffs

From the muslin, cut:
   1 square, 21" x 21", for lining

Assembling the Garden Neck Roll

1. Arrange the 4" squares in 5 rows of 5 squares each. Sew the squares together in rows and press the seams in opposite directions from row to row.

2. Layer the neck roll top with batting and the muslin lining. I like to sprinkle a few tablespoons of dried lavender between the lining and the batting for an added garden-scent effect. Adding lavender is easy to do if you lightly spray the lining with the basting adhesive first, sprinkle the lavender over the adhesive, and then add the batting. Add a light coat of adhesive to the top of the batting and then position the patchwork on top. Smooth out any wrinkles.

3. If available, use an even-feed foot or a walking foot on your sewing machine to machine quilt in the ditch of all seams or as desired. Trim pillow top even with lining.

4. Add the 4½" x 20½" end cuffs and press the seams toward the cuffs.

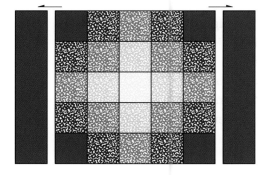

5. Stitch the long edges together with right sides facing. Finger-press the seam open and whip-stitch the seam allowance edges to the cuff at each end to keep them in place. Turn the patchwork tube right side out.

6. Push the cuff pieces inside the tube and top-stitch ⅛" from each folded edge.

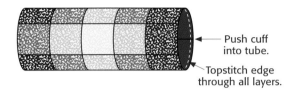

Push cuff into tube.

Topstitch edge through all layers.

7. Pull the cuffs back out of the tube.

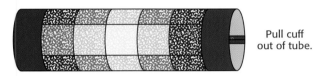

Pull cuff out of tube.

8. Turn under and press ¼" at each cuff end. Turn under ¾" and press. Stitch along the inner fold at each end of the pillow tube to create casings. Leave a ½"-long opening in each one. With a safety pin or bodkin, thread an 18"-long piece of heavy cord through each casing.

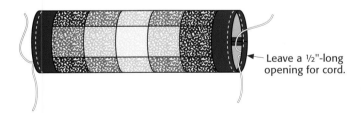

Leave a ½"-long opening for cord.

9. Stuff the tube with polyester fiberfill. Pull the cord tight and tie into a knot to close the openings. Hide the cord ends by pushing them through the tiny opening. Hand stitch the opening closed for added security.

10. Optional: Add a large decorative button at each end of the pillow if desired.

Garden Pillow

BY KARLA ALEXANDER, 19½" x 19½"
Like the neck roll, this pretty pillow was made from leftover blocks and is lavender scented.

Materials for Garden Pillow

Yardage is based on 42"-wide fabric, with 40" of usable width after preshrinking. Refer to "Cutting Crazy Blocks for Garden Neck Roll and Garden Pillow" on page 25 for instructions regarding the floral 4" squares listed below.

8 light floral 4" squares for pillow top
8 medium-light floral 4" squares for pillow top
8 dark floral 4" squares for pillow top
¼ yd. dark floral for corner squares and sashing strips
Two 21½" x 21½" pieces of muslin for lining
⅝ yd. fabric for pillow back
Two 21½" x 21½" pieces of batting
Polyester fiberfill or 20" pillow form*
¼ cup dried lavender (optional)
Spray-basting adhesive (optional)
*A form that is slightly larger than the finished pillow size ensures a snug-fitting pillow cover.

Cutting for Garden Pillow

All measurements include ¼"-wide seam allowances.

From the ¼ yd. of dark floral, cut:

4 squares, each 5" x 5", for corner squares

4 rectangles, each 1½" x 11", for sashing strips

From the fabric for pillow back, cut:

1 square, 20" x 20"

Assembling the Garden Pillow Top

1. Arrange the 4" squares in the 5 rows shown and sew together in rows. Press the seams in opposite directions from row to row.

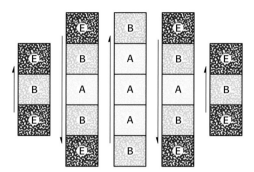

2. Sew the 3 center rows together and press the seams in one direction. Sew the sashing strips to the outer and center block sections as shown and press the seams toward the sashing strips. Add corner squares to the outer block units and press the seams toward the squares. Sew the resulting units together to complete the pillow top. Press the seams in one direction.

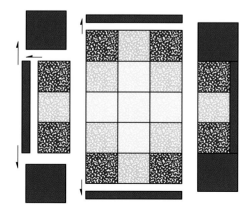

3. Layer the pillow top with batting and the muslin lining. I like to sprinkle a few table-spoons of dried lavender between the lining and the batting for an added garden-scent effect. Lightly spray the lining with the basting adhesive first, then sprinkle the lavender over the adhesive, and finally add the batting. Add a light coat of adhesive to the top of the batting and then position the patchwork on top. Smooth out any wrinkles. Repeat this process with the remaining piece of batting, muslin lining, and pillow back.

4. Machine quilt horizontally and vertically in the ditch along the seams of the pillow top. Use a walking foot if you have one. Mark and quilt a 2" horizontal and vertical grid on the pillow back, quilting by machine, if desired.

Finishing the Garden Pillow

1. Machine stitch ⅜" from one edge of the pillow top and the pillow back to strengthen the pillow opening edge.

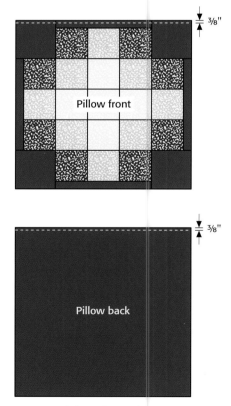

Stitch ⅜" from edge
to strengthen pillow opening.

2. Using an arc template made with the pattern at lower right, mark all 4 corners on the wrong side of the pillow top and back. Carefully trim the batting and lining along the lines, exposing the wrong side of the patchwork and the pillow back.

3. With the right sides together, pin and sew the pillow top and back together, leaving an 8" opening at the edge with the reinforcement stitching (see step 1).

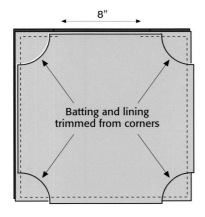

Batting and lining trimmed from corners

4. Place one hand into one corner of the pillow top and spread your fingers inside to open the corner. Finger-press the adjacent seam allowances open for an inch or so and align them to form a point. With a strong, doubled thread, do a small gathering stitch along the arc line. Pull the gathering threads tight and wrap them around the gathers several times. Take a few stitches to secure the stitch. Repeat at the remaining corners. Do not trim or clip the corners. You need the bulk to fill out the soft corners when the pillow is turned right side out.

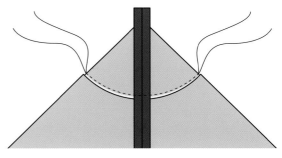

Gathering Stitches at Corners

5. Turn the pillow right side out and stuff with polyester fiberfill or a pillow form.

6. Turn the edges of the opening in along the stitched edges and hand sew the opening closed with small stitches.

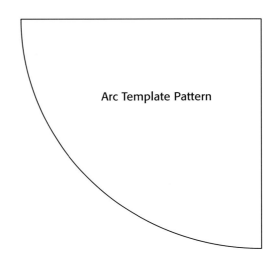

Arc Template Pattern

By Karla Alexander

Luscious velvet is the perfect companion for the simplicity of a four-segment Crazy block.
This quilt is a fast and easy project, and the results are simply luxurious.

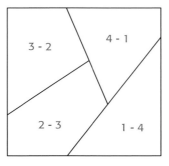

Block Cutting and Sewing Guide
Cut Size: 12" x 12"

MATERIALS

Fabric widths may vary from 45" to 60". Do not preshrink.

⅜ yd.* *each* of 12 assorted woven velvets and/or velveteens for Crazy blocks

½ yd. woven velvet or velveteen for binding

3 yds. woven velvet or velveteen for backing

50" x 68" piece of batting

Most stores tear velvet rather than cut it. To be sure you have a large enough strip from which to cut 12" squares, it's best to purchase ⅜ yard.

Note: Read "Tips for Sewing with Velvet" at right before you begin. This quilt is very fast and easy to make—with luscious results. Sewing on velvet is different from sewing on cotton quilting fabric, but don't be afraid of using it. Just have fun and go for it. Remember, you're making a Crazy quilt to cuddle under, not a fancy dress that requires hours of perfect sewing! This soft, lightweight throw will delight you in the end!

TIPS FOR SEWING WITH VELVET

▸ To avoid flattening the luxurious napped velvet surface, don't put the weight of the iron on the fabric; finger-press instead. You can finger-press more easily if you hold a steam iron just above the seam to coax a little steam into it first.

▸ Velvet can be rather slippery, so use pins to control it while you stitch. It's a good idea to use a slightly wider seam allowance than the normal ¼" patchwork seam due to the increased bulk. Consider using a walking foot to help control seam slippage while you stitch.

▸ Although velvet and velveteen both have a nap, you don't need to pay attention to it in Crazy blocks. The color variations that result by turning the squares so the nap is different add more interest to the finished blocks.

▸ Velvet makes great single-fold binding, too. For ⅝"-wide finished binding, cut 2¾"-wide straight-grain strips and stitch the strips to the quilt top using a ⅝"-wide seam. Turn the binding to the quilt wrong side, turn under the raw edges, and slipstitch in place as you would any other fabric binding strips.

CUTTING

All measurements include ¼"-wide seam allowances. Cut or tear all strips across the fabric width (crosswise grain).

From each of the 12 woven velvets and/or velveteens for Crazy blocks, cut or tear:

  1 strip, 12" wide, across the fabric width for a total of 12 strips. Crosscut or tear each strip into 3 squares, 12" x 12", for a total of 36 squares.

From the woven velvet or velveteen for binding, cut or tear:

  6 strips, each 2¾" wide

PIECING THE CRAZY BLOCKS

1. Arrange and stack the 12" squares into 4 decks of 8 squares each. Each deck should contain 8 different velvet fabrics. Secure each deck with a pin through all layers until ready to sew.
2. Referring to "Making the Crazy Blocks" on page 9, make 36 four-segment whole blocks. Trim the blocks to 9" x 9".

Note: If you use a slightly wider seam than ¼" (no more than ⅜") as recommended in the tip box on page 31, you will still have blocks of the correct size. However, it's a good idea to measure all your finished velvet blocks to find out if there is a size discrepancy. If there is, determine the size that you can trim all the blocks to and that is closest to the required 9" cut size, and trim the blocks to this size.

ASSEMBLING THE QUILT TOP

1. Arrange the blocks in 7 horizontal rows of 5 blocks each. Pin and sew the blocks together in rows and finger-press the seams open (see "Tips for Sewing with Velvet" on page 31).
2. Sew the rows together to complete the quilt top and finger-press the seams open.

FINISHING YOUR QUILT

1. Divide the backing fabric crosswise to make 2 panels, each approximately 54" long. Remove the selvages and join the pieces at the long edges to make the backing. Press the seam to one side.
2. Layer the quilt top with batting and backing, with the backing seam running parallel to the short edges of the quilt top. To baste, use basting spray adhesive for best results (see page 18).
3. If available, use a walking foot or the even-feed feature on your machine to machine quilt. Or, hand quilt if desired.
4. Trim the backing and batting even with the quilt-top edges and bind with velvet as described in "Tips for Sewing with Velvet" on page 31.
5. Add a label to the back, if desired, and cuddle up!

American Muster

By Karla Alexander

"American Muster" was designed while our son Kelly came home for a quick
two-week break from the navy before being deployed to a ship in Guam.

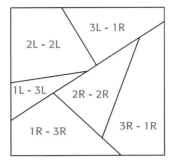

Block Cutting and Sewing Guide
Cut Size: 11" x 11"

MATERIALS

Yardage is based on 42"-wide fabric, with 40" of usable width after preshrinking.

⅜ yd. *each* of 12 assorted red-white-and-blue
   prints for Crazy blocks
¼ yd. gold for inner border 1
⅓ yd. red for inner border 2
⅓ yd. white for inner border 3
⅞ yd. blue for outer border
⅝ yd. fabric for binding
3½ yds. fabric for backing
59" x 76" piece of batting

CUTTING

All measurements include ¼"-wide seam allowances.
Cut all strips across the fabric width (crosswise grain).
From *each* of the 12 prints for Crazy blocks, cut:
   1 strip, 11" wide, for a total of 12 strips.
      Crosscut each strip into 3 squares, 11" x 11",
      for a total of 36 squares.
From the gold for inner border 1, cut:
   6 strips, each 1" wide
From the red for inner border 2, cut:
   6 strips, each 1½" wide
From the white for inner border 3, cut:
   6 strips, each 1½" wide

From the blue for outer border, cut:
   7 strips, each 4" wide
From the binding fabric, cut:
   7 strips, each 2½" wide

PIECING THE CRAZY BLOCKS

1. Arrange the 11" squares in 4 decks of 9 squares each. Each deck should contain 9 different prints. Secure the decks with a pin through all layers until ready to sew.
2. Referring to "Making the Crazy Blocks" on page 9, make 36 six-segment two-sided blocks. Trim the blocks to 9" x 9". You will have 1 extra block. (I make an extra block so I have more options for arranging the blocks for the quilt top).

ASSEMBLING THE QUILT TOP

1. Arrange the blocks in 7 horizontal rows of 5 blocks each and sew the blocks together in rows. Press the seams in opposite directions from row to row.
2. Sew the rows together and press the seams in one direction.
3. Sew the borders to the quilt top, referring to "Adding the Borders" on page 16.

FINISHING YOUR QUILT

1. Divide the backing fabric crosswise into 2 panels, each approximately 60" long. Remove the selvages and join the long edges to make the backing. Press the seam to one side.
2. Layer the quilt top with batting and backing, with the backing seam parallel to the short edges of the quilt top. Baste the layers together using your favorite method (see page 18).
3. Hand or machine quilt as desired.
4. Trim the backing and batting even with the quilt-top edges and bind the quilt (see page 20).
5. Add a label and enjoy your finished quilt. Or send it off to be loved by someone dear to you who is serving in the armed forces.

Crazy Hearts

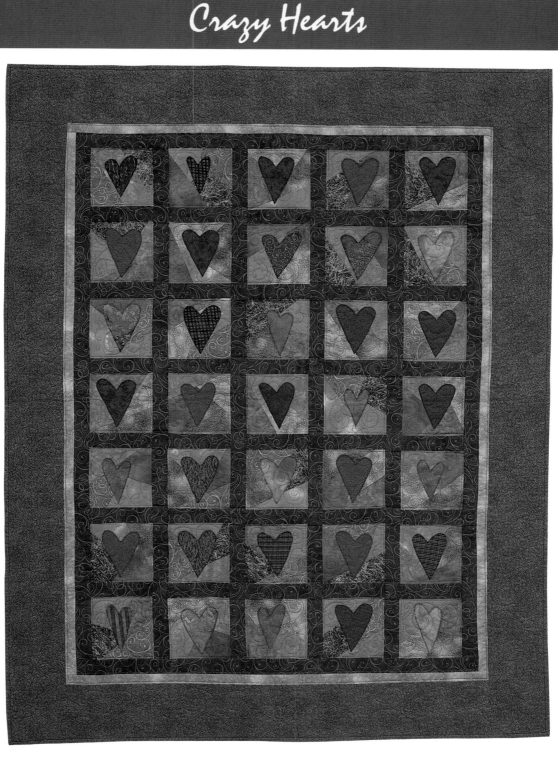

BY KARLA ALEXANDER

Twice each year I teach at a quilting retreat in the rolling hills of Silver Falls, Oregon, with my quilting pal Sue Ann Suderman. The colorful fall leaves that I collected while teaching at the retreat this past fall provided inspiration for the brilliant reds and greens in "Crazy Hearts." I begged and borrowed enough red and purple scraps from each retreat attendee to make this special quilt—a tribute to the magnificence of fall and the wonderful people at the retreat.

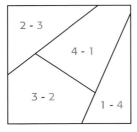

Block Cutting and Sewing Guide
Cut Size: 8" x 8"

MATERIALS

Yardage is based on 42"-wide fabric, with 40" of usable width after preshrinking.

¼ yd. *each* of 9 different green prints for Crazy blocks

35 different squares ranging in color from purple to red, each 5" x 5", for heart appliqués

1 yd. purple tone-on-tone print for sashing

⅓ yd. medium purple for inner border

1¼ yds. dark purple for outer border

4 yds. fabric for backing

⅝ yd. dark purple for binding

55" x 69" piece of batting

2 yds. fusible web

CUTTING

All measurements include ¼"-wide seam allowances. Cut all strips across the fabric width (crosswise grain).

From *each* of the 9 prints for Crazy blocks, cut:

1 strip, 8" wide, for a total of 9 strips; crosscut each strip into 4 squares, 8" x 8", for a total of 36 squares.

From the sashing fabric, cut:

14 strips, each 2" wide; crosscut 5 of the strips into 30 sashing strips, each 2" x 6". Set the remaining long strips aside for step 4 in "Assembling the Quilt Top."

From the inner border fabric, cut:

5 strips, each 1½" wide

From the outer border fabric, cut:

6 strips, each 6" wide

From the binding fabric, cut:

6 strips, each 2½" wide

PIECING AND APPLIQUÉING THE CRAZY BLOCKS

1. Arrange the 8" squares into 4 decks of 9 squares each. Each deck should contain 9 different prints. Secure each deck with a pin through all layers until ready to sew.

2. Referring to "Making the Crazy Blocks" on page 9, make 36 four-segment whole blocks. Trim the blocks to 6" x 6". You will have 1 extra block. (I make an extra block so I have more options for arranging the blocks for the quilt top.)

3. Refer to "Adding Appliqués" on page 16. Use the template pattern on page 37 and the 5" x 5" squares to make heart appliqués. Position and fuse the appliqués to the blocks made in step 2, referring to the quilt photo for placement.

ASSEMBLING THE QUILT TOP

1. Arrange the blocks in 7 horizontal rows of 5 blocks each. Turn the blocks until you are satisfied with the layout.

2. Sew a 2" x 6" sashing strip to the bottom edge of each block, with the exception of the blocks in the lowest horizontal row. Press the seams toward the sashing. Sew the blocks together in 5 vertical rows. Press.

3. Sew the remaining 9 sashing strips together to make 1 long strip.

4. Measure the pieced vertical rows through the centers and determine the average length of the rows. From the long sashing strip, cut 6 sashing strips to that measurement. Arrange the sashing with the block strips and sew together. Press the seams toward the sashing strips.

1. Divide the backing fabric crosswise into 2 panels, each approximately 60" long. Remove the selvages and sew 2 long edges together to make the backing. Press the seam to one side.

2. Layer the quilt top with batting and backing, with the backing seam parallel to the short edges of the quilt top. Baste the layers together using your favorite method (see page 18).

3. Hand or machine quilt as desired. I used free-motion, swirling stipple stitching on the blocks and in the borders, and I quilted in the ditch along all the vertical and horizontal seamlines.

4. Trim the backing and batting even with the quilt-top edges and bind the quilt (see page 20).

5. Add a label to the back and enjoy your new quilt.

5. Measure the quilt top through its horizontal center. From the remaining long sashing strip, cut 2 sashing strips to that measurement. Sew a sashing strip to the top and bottom edges of the quilt top; press toward the sashing strips.

Heart Template Pattern
Cut 35 assorted purples and reds.

*Use this pattern as a guide
to cut hearts, varying
each one slightly as you cut.*

6. Sew the inner border strips together to make 1 long strip. Repeat with the outer border strips. Add the inner border and then the outer border, following the directions for "Adding the Borders" on page 16. Press all seams toward the border strips as you go.

Big, Fat Comforter

By Karla Alexander

Made from twenty oversized blocks cut from twenty different fat quarters, this quilt almost sews itself!
Change the finished quilt-top size by simply increasing or reducing the number of fat quarters.

<table>
<tr><td>

Sizes and Block Requirements

Finished Size: 62" x 76"

Finished Crazy Block Size: 15½" x 15½"

Crazy Block Requirements: 20 Six-Segment Whole Blocks

</td></tr>
</table>

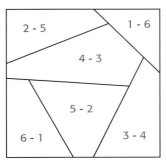

Block Sewing and Cutting Guide
Cut Size: 17" x 17"

MATERIALS

1 fat quarter (18" x 20" piece) *each* of 20 different contrasting fabrics for Crazy blocks

4½ yds. of 42"-wide fabric (40" after preshrinking) for backing

24 assorted buttons to coordinate or contrast with your fabrics

66" x 80" piece of high-loft polyester batting

CUTTING AND PIECING THE CRAZY BLOCKS

All measurements include ¼"-wide seam allowances.

1. For the blocks, trim each of the 20 fat quarters into a 17" square.

2. Arrange the 17" squares into 2 decks of 10 different prints each. Secure each deck with a pin through all layers until ready to sew.

3. Referring to "Making the Crazy Blocks" on page 9, make 20 six-segment whole blocks. Trim the blocks to 16" square.

ASSEMBLING THE COMFORTER TOP

1. Arrange the blocks in 5 horizontal rows with 4 blocks in each. Play with the blocks, moving and turning them, until you are satisfied with the layout. Try to arrange the blocks so that identical prints don't end up side by side in the quilt top.

2. Pin and sew the blocks together in 5 horizontal rows and press the seams in opposite directions from row to row. Sew the rows together and press the seams in one direction.

FINISHING YOUR COMFORTER

1. Divide the backing fabric crosswise into 2 panels, each approximately 80" long. Remove the selvages and sew the pieces together along 2 long edges to make the backing. Press the seam to one side.

2. Place the backing right side up on top of the batting layer. Place the quilt top facedown on the backing. Use long quilting pins to hold the layers together, making sure that all layers are smooth and wrinkle-free. Place the pins 2" from and parallel to the raw edges all around.

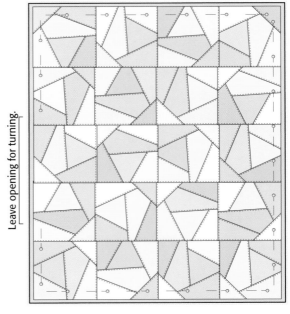

Wrong Side of Quilt Top

3. With the batting on the bottom, stitch the layers together, using a walking foot or the even-feed feature on your sewing machine. Begin sewing along one of the short sides, a few blocks away from a corner. Sew around all 4 sides of the comforter, leaving an 18" opening on the long side.

Note: I use a ⅜"-wide seam allowance to make it easier to stitch accurately through the bulky layers.

4. Trim the backing and batting even with the comforter top. Turn the comforter right side out through the opening on the long side. Use a blunt-pointed object such as a wooden or plastic point turner (check the notions section at your local quilt shop for this) to push the corners out. Whipstitch the opening closed.

5. Arrange the comforter on a large, flat surface and smooth out any wrinkles with your hands. Pin the layers together, placing long quilting pins at the block intersections. Machine quilt in the seamlines at each intersection, extending the stitching 4" in each direction. Center a button in each square and hand sew in place through all the layers. Also sew a button at each of the 4 corners of the quilt top.

Note: Do not try to machine quilt along the entire length of each seamline because the quilt edges will roll to the front or the back and show.

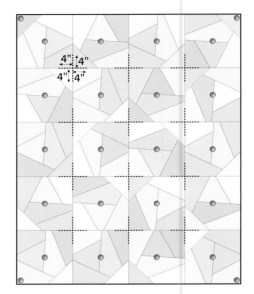

Quilting Design and Button Placement

Crazy Eights

BY LISA ENCABO

"Crazy Eights" is the perfect fat-quarter quilt to make from your favorite collection of beautiful batiks; you only need 8 for the body of the quilt, with extras thrown in for good measure in the setting triangles and borders.

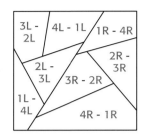

Block Cutting and Sewing Guide
Cut Size: 17" x 17"

MATERIALS

Yardage is based on 42"-wide fabric, with 40" of usable width after preshrinking.

1 fat quarter *each* of 8 different batiks for Crazy blocks

¾ yd. *each* of 2 different batiks for setting triangles

⅜ yd. fabric for inner border

1⅓ yds. fabric for outer border

3⅝ yds. fabric for backing

⅝ yd. fabric for binding

62" x 79" piece of batting

CUTTING

All measurements include ¼"-wide seam allowances.
Cut all strips across the fabric width (crosswise grain).

From *each* of the 8 fat quarters for Crazy blocks, cut:

1 square, 17" x 17"

From *each* of the 2 batiks for setting triangles, cut:

1 square, 23" x 23"; cut each square twice diagonally to yield 8 side setting triangles. (You will have 2 left over.)

1 square, 12" x 12"; cut each square once diagonally to yield 4 corner setting triangles.

From the inner border fabric, cut:

6 strips, each 2" wide

From the outer border fabric, cut:

7 strips, each 6½" wide

From the binding fabric, cut:

7 strips, each 2½" wide

PIECING THE CRAZY BLOCKS

1. Arrange the 17" squares into 1 deck of 8 different batiks. Secure the deck with a pin through all layers until ready to sew.

2. Referring to "Making the Crazy Blocks" on page 9, make 8 eight-segment two-sided blocks. Trim the blocks to 15" x 15".

ASSEMBLING THE QUILT TOP

1. Arrange the blocks and corner setting triangles in diagonal rows. Play with the blocks, moving and turning them, until you are satisfied with the arrangement. Try to arrange the blocks so identical prints are not side by side in the completed layout.

2. Sew the blocks and side setting triangles together in diagonal rows and press as directed by the arrows. Add the corner setting triangles and press the seams toward the triangles.

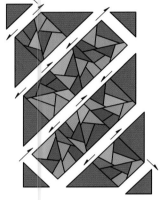

3. Sew the strips for the inner border together to make 1 long strip. Cut the inner border strips to size and sew them to the quilt top as directed in "Adding the Borders" on page 16. Repeat with the outer border strips.

FINISHING YOUR QUILT

1. Divide the backing fabric crosswise into 2 panels, each approximately 64" long. Remove the selvages and sew the pieces together along 2 long edges to make the backing. Press the seam open.

2. Layer the quilt top with batting and backing, with the backing seam parallel to the short edges of the quilt top. Baste the layers together with your favorite method (see page 18).

3. Hand or machine quilt as desired.

4. Trim the backing and batting even with the quilt-top edges and bind the quilt (see page 20).

BY KARLA ALEXANDER

Crazy blocks mix well with preprinted squares or squares fussy cut from conversation prints.
This is an especially nice quilt to make for a baby gift.

Sizes and Block Requirements

Finished Size: 34" x 43"

Finished Crazy Block Size: 4½" x 4½"

Crazy Block Requirements: 49 Four-Segment
  Whole Blocks

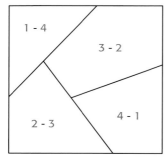

Block Cutting and Sewing Guide
Cut Size: 7" x 7"

MATERIALS

Yardage is based on 42"-wide fabric, with 40" of usable width after preshrinking.

¼ yd. *each* of 10 different prints for Crazy blocks

14 preprinted 5" squares*

⅓ yd. fabric for sashing

4 squares, each 2" x 2", for cornerstones

1½ yds. fabric for backing

⅜ yd. fabric for binding

38" x 47" piece of batting

You can also use 5" squares of your favorite fabrics or 5" squares with photo transfers. If you prefer to use squares with the same preprinted design in each square—a particular bunny, for example—you will need to calculate your own yardage because the size and spacing of designs varies from fabric to fabric. You may need more than 1 yard of the preprinted fabric. If you prefer to use an all-over printed design for the squares, you will need only ⅓ yard of the fabric to cut 14 squares, each 5" x 5".

CUTTING

All measurements include ¼"-wide seam allowances. Cut all strips across the fabric width (crosswise grain).

From *each* of the 10 prints for Crazy blocks, cut:

  1 strip, 7" wide, for a total of 10 strips; crosscut each strip into 5 squares, 7" x 7", for a total of 50 squares.

Trim all preprinted squares to measure 5" x 5".

From the sashing fabric, cut:

  4 strips, each 2" wide; crosscut strips into 2 strips, each 2" x 32", and 2 strips, each 2" x 23". From the remainder of the strips, cut 8 strips, each 2" x 5".

From the binding fabric, cut:

  5 strips, each 2½" wide

PIECING THE CRAZY BLOCKS

1. Arrange the 7" squares in 5 decks of 10 each. Each deck should contain 10 different prints. Secure each deck with a pin through all layers until ready to sew. (You will have an extra block.)

2. Referring to "Making the Crazy Blocks" on page 9, make 50 four-segment whole blocks. Trim the blocks to 5" x 5".

ASSEMBLING THE QUILT TOP

1. Arrange the Crazy blocks, 5" preprinted squares, cornerstones, and sashing strips as shown. You'll have 1 extra Crazy block, so substitute if necessary, moving and turning the blocks until you are satisfied with the arrangement. Try to arrange the blocks so identical prints are not next to each other in the Crazy block border strips.

2. Sew the blocks and squares in the center panel together and press the seams in opposite directions from row to row. Sew the rows together and press the seams in one direction.

3. Sew the vertical border blocks together and press the seams in one direction. Sew a 2" x 32" sashing strip to each border strip and press the seam toward the sashing strip. Join the border-and-sashing strips to the quilt-top center and press the seams toward the sashing.

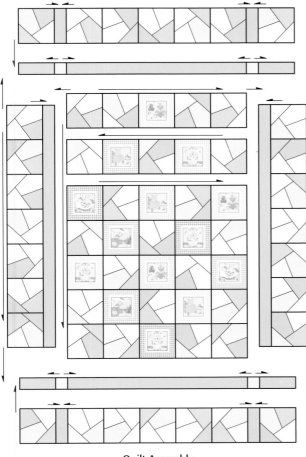

Quilt Assembly

4. Sew the horizontal border blocks and 2" x 5" sashing strips together. Sew the cornerstones and remaining sashing strips together as shown. Press all seams toward the sashing strips.

5. Sew a horizontal sashing strip with cornerstones to each pieced border from step 4. Press the seams toward the sashing strips. Sew the horizontal borders to the quilt top. Press the seams toward the sashing strips.

FINISHING YOUR QUILT

1. Layer the quilt top with batting and backing. Baste the layers together with your favorite method (see page 18).

2. Hand or machine quilt as desired.

3. Trim the backing and batting even with the quilt-top edges and bind the quilt (see page 20).

4. Add a label to the back and enjoy your new quilt!

BY KARLA ALEXANDER
Baby will fall asleep on these puffy clouds and twinkly stars surrounded by a Crazy block border.

Sizes and Block Requirements

Finished Size: 38" x 51"

Finished Crazy Block Size: 6½" x 6½"

Finished Patchwork Block Size (in Patchwork Quilt Center): 4½" x 4½"

Crazy Block Requirements: 24 Five-Segment Whole Blocks

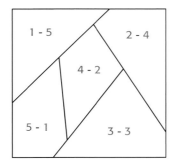

Block Cutting and Sewing Guide
Cut Size: 9" x 9"

MATERIALS

Yardage is based on 42"-wide fabric, with 40" of usable width after preshrinking.

¼ yd. *each* of 6 different blue prints for patchwork quilt center

⅓ yd. *each* of 6 different bright prints for Crazy blocks in outer border

⅓ yd. fabric for inner border

Assorted blue scraps for star appliqués

⅛ yd. white for cloud appliqués

10" square of yellow print for moon

1⅝ yds. fabric for backing

⅜ yd. fabric for binding

1½ yds. fusible web

42" x 55" piece of batting

CUTTING

All measurements include ¼"-wide seam allowances. Cut all strips across the fabric width (crosswise grain).

From *each* of the 6 blue prints for patchwork quilt center, cut:

1 strip, 5" wide, for a total of 6 strips

From *each* of the 6 bright prints for Crazy blocks in outer border, cut:

1 strip, 9" wide, for a total of 6; crosscut each strip into 4 squares, 9" x 9", for a total of 24 squares.

From the inner border fabric, cut:

4 strips, each 2½" wide

From the binding fabric, cut:

5 strips, each 2½" wide

MAKING THE PATCHWORK QUILT CENTER

1. Arrange the 5"-wide blue strips in the desired order and sew together to create 1 large strip set. As you add each strip to the strip unit, stitch the new seam in the opposite direction from the previous one (as indicated by the arrows). Press the seams in one direction.

2. From the strip set, crosscut 7 sections, each 5" wide.

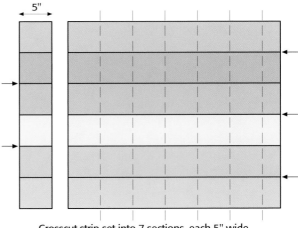

Crosscut strip set into 7 sections, each 5" wide.

3. Sew the 7 sections together to make 1 long strip.
4. Remove the stitching between squares as needed to create 5 rows of 8 blocks each. Arrange the 8-block strips in 5 vertical rows. Play around with the strips, trading one row for another and turning them upside down if necessary until you are satisfied with the arrangement.

Note: To make it easier to join the strips, re-press the seams in alternating rows so all seams are in opposing directions from row to row.

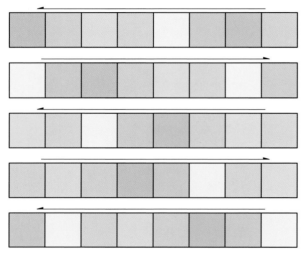

Separate the long pieced strip
into 5 strips of 8 squares each.
Re-press seams as needed so direction
alternates from row to row.

5. Sew the rows together to create the patchwork center of the quilt top and press the seams in one direction.

PIECING THE CRAZY BLOCKS

1. Arrange the 9" squares into 4 decks of 6 squares each. Each deck should contain 6 different bright prints. Secure each deck with a pin through all layers until ready to sew.
2. Referring to "Making the Crazy Blocks" on page 9, make 24 five-segment whole blocks. Trim the blocks to 7" x 7".

COMPLETING THE QUILT TOP

1. Sew the inner border strips together to make 1 long piece. Trim to size and sew to the patchwork center of the quilt top, following the directions for "Adding the Borders" on page 16. Press the seams toward the border strips.
2. Arrange the quilt top on a large, flat surface and position the Crazy blocks around the outside edges to form a frame. Move, turn, and trade the block positions until you are satisfied with the arrangement.
3. Sew the Crazy blocks for the side outer border strips together with a scant ¼"-wide seam allowance (a little less than ¼"). The narrower seam allowance ensures that the border strips will be long enough to fit the quilt top. Sew the side outer border strips to the quilt top and press the seams toward the inner border.

4. Using a normal ¼"-wide seam allowance, sew the Crazy blocks for the top and bottom outer border strips together. Measure the finished outer border strips and adjust the seam allowances if necessary to make them fit the quilt-top edges. Sew the strips to the quilt top and press the seams toward the inner border.

Quilt Assembly

ADDING THE APPLIQUÉS

1. Use the appliqué template patterns on pages 73–74 and refer to "Adding Appliqués" on page 16 to prepare the appliqués.
2. Position and fuse appliqués in place, referring to the quilt assembly diagram at left for placement.

FINISHING YOUR QUILT

1. Layer the quilt top with batting and backing. Baste the layers together using your favorite method (see page 18).
2. Hand or machine quilt as desired.
3. Trim the backing and batting even with the quilt-top edges and bind the quilt (see page 20).
4. Add a label to the back before you wrap a sweet baby in the new quilt.

Jungle Cover

BY KARLA ALEXANDER

My "adopted" chameleon, Lincoln, lives at a local pet store, where I visit him often.
Now I can see him even more since his likeness resides permanently in a corner of this jungle quilt.

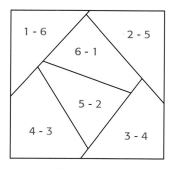

Block Cutting and Sewing Guide
Cut Size: 11" x 11"

MATERIALS

Yardage is based on 42"-wide fabric, with 40" of usable width after preshrinking.

⅜ yd. *each* of 6 different burnt red and orange fabrics for Crazy blocks

⅜ yd. *each* of 6 different brown and black fabrics for Crazy blocks

⅜ yd. *each* of 6 different green fabrics for Crazy blocks

½ yd. dark brown for inner border

1⅛ yds. medium brown for outer border

18" square of green for chameleon

⅛ yd. *each* of 2 different green and brown fabrics for chameleon stripes, eye, and branch

2 yds. fusible web

⅝ yd. fabric for binding

5⅓ yds. fabric for backing

66" x 91" piece of batting

CUTTING

All measurements include ¼"-wide seam allowances. Cut all strips across the fabric width (crosswise grain).

From *each* of the fabrics for Crazy blocks, cut:

1 strip, 11" wide, for a total of 18 strips; crosscut each strip into 3 squares, 11" x 11", for a total of 54 squares.

From the dark brown for inner border, cut:

7 strips, each 1¾" wide

From the medium brown for outer border, cut:

8 strips, each 4½" wide

From the binding fabric, cut:

8 strips, each 2½" wide

PIECING THE CRAZY BLOCKS

1. Arrange the 11" squares into 6 decks of 9 each. Each deck should contain 9 different fabrics. Secure each deck with a pin through all layers until ready to sew.

2. Referring to "Making the Crazy Blocks" on page 9, make 54 six-segment whole blocks. Trim the blocks to 9" x 9".

ASSEMBLING THE QUILT TOP

1. Arrange 9 horizontal rows of 6 Crazy blocks each. Play with the blocks, moving and turning them until you are satisfied with the arrangement. Try to arrange the blocks so identical prints are not side by side in the finished quilt layout.

2. Sew the blocks together in horizontal rows and press the seams in opposite directions from row to row. Sew the rows together and press the seams in one direction

3. Sew the strips for the inner border together to make 1 long strip. Trim to size and sew to the quilt as directed in "Adding the Borders" on page 16. Press the seams toward the border strips. Repeat with the outer border strips. Press the seams toward the outer border strips.

ADDING THE APPLIQUÉS

1. Using the appliqué template patterns on page 75 and referring to "Adding Appliqués" on page 16, prepare the appliqués.
2. Referring to the chameleon appliqué templates and the illustration below, position and fuse the appliqués in place on the quilt top.

FINISHING YOUR QUILT

1. Divide the backing fabric crosswise into 2 panels, each approximately 93" long. Remove the selvages and sew the pieces together along 2 long edges to make the backing. Press the seam to one side.
2. Layer the quilt top with batting and backing, with the backing seam parallel to the short edges of the quilt top. Baste the layers together with your favorite method (see page 18).
3. Hand or machine quilt as desired.
4. Trim the backing and batting even with the quilt-top edges and bind the quilt (see page 20).
5. Add a label to the back and enjoy your new quilt.

Midnight Hour

BY KARLA ALEXANDER. QUILTED BY SUE ANN SUDERMAN.
"Midnight Hour" is a calm reflection of frequent rainy nights in Oregon.
The full moon glows through the branches of the ever-abundant Douglas fir.

Sizes and Block Requirements

Finished Size: 67" x 87"

Finished Crazy Block Size: 7½" x 7½"

Crazy Block Requirements: 50 Five-Segment Whole Blocks

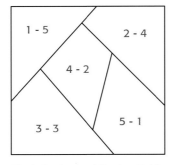

Block Cutting and Sewing Guide
Cut Size: 10" x 10"

MATERIALS

Yardage is based on 42"-wide fabric, with 40" of usable width after preshrinking.

⅛ yd. dark print for center medallion border

⅓ yd. dark fabric or a 10" dark fabric square for center medallion background

½ yd. or a 14" square of medium purple-and-turquoise batik for center medallion triangles

¼ yd. purple for center medallion checkerboard border

¼ yd. green for center medallion checkerboard border

¼ yd. orange for center medallion outer border

⅓ yd. *each* of 13 different prints for Crazy blocks

¾ yd. teal print for side and corner setting triangles

Assorted orange, brown, and green scraps for frog and dragonfly appliqués

⅓ yd. purple print for inner border

1⅜ yds. teal print for outer border

5¼ yds. fabric for backing

¾ yd. fabric for binding

71" x 91" piece of batting

1½ yds. fusible web

CUTTING

All measurements include ¼"-wide seam allowances. Cut all strips across the fabric width (crosswise grain).

From the dark print for center medallion border, cut:
2 strips, each 1¾" wide; crosscut the strips into 2 strips, each 1¾" x 10", and 2 strips, each 1¾" x 12½".

From the dark fabric for center medallion, cut:
One 10" square

From the medium purple-and-turquoise batik for center medallion triangles, cut:
One 14" square; cut square twice diagonally to yield 4 triangles.

From the purple for center medallion checkerboard border, cut:
4 strips, each 1½" wide

From the green for center medallion checkerboard border, cut:
4 strips, each 1½" wide

From the orange for center medallion outer border, cut:
2 strips, each 2" wide (directions for additional cutting in medallion construction steps)

From *each* of the 13 prints for Crazy blocks, cut:
1 strip, 10" wide, for a total of 13 strips. Crosscut each strip into 4 squares, 10" x 10", for a total of 52 squares.

From the teal print for setting triangles, cut:
2 strips, each 12" wide; crosscut the strips into 5 squares, each 12" x 12". Cut each square twice diagonally to yield 20 side setting triangles.

2 squares, each 7" x 7". Cut each square once diagonally to yield 4 corner setting triangles.

From the purple print for inner border, cut:
7 strips, each 1½" wide

From the teal print for outer border, cut:
8 strips, each 6" wide

From the binding fabric, cut:
8 strips, each 2½" wide

MAKING THE CENTER MEDALLION

1. Sew a 1¾" x 10" dark-print border strip to opposite sides of the 10" square of dark fabric. Press the seams toward the border strips. Add the 1¾" x 12½" dark-print border strips to the remaining edges. Press.

2. Fold the square in quarters to find and pin mark the center of each edge. Fold the long edge of each medium purple-and-turquoise triangle in half to find and pin mark the center. Matching centers, stitch triangles to opposite sides of the center medallion square and press the seams toward the triangles. Add the remaining medium purple-and-turquoise triangles in the same manner.

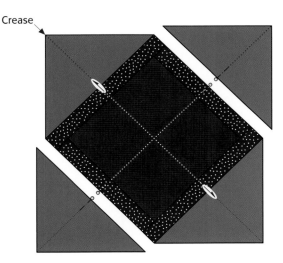
Crease

3. Alternate 2 purple and 2 green 1½"-wide strips and sew together to create a strip set. Press the seams toward the purple strips. Repeat with the remaining 2 purple and 2 green strips. Cut each strip set into 3 equal segments—approximately 13" long.

Make 2 checkerboard strip sets.
Cut each into 3 equal segments.

4. Sew 3 of the strip set segments together and press the seams toward the purple fabric. Repeat with the remaining 3 strip set segments. Cut each of the resulting strip sets in half.

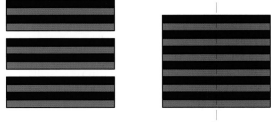
Make 2.
Cut each in half.

5. Sew the halves together in pairs, side by side, to make 2 new strip sets, each 7" x 24½".

6. Rotary cut 4 strips, 1½" x 24½", from each strip set made in step 5. You should have 8 strips, with 24 squares in each strip.

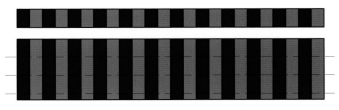
Crosscut into 4 strips for checkerboard border.

7. Remove 7 squares from the right end of 2 strips and 7 from the left end of 2 strips so that each strip has 17 squares.

Remove 7 squares from the right end of 2 strip sets.

Remove 7 squares from the left end of 2 strip sets.

8. Remove 3 squares from the right end of 2 strips and 3 squares from the left end of the other 2 remaining strips so that each strip has only 21 squares.

Remove 3 squares from the right end of 2 strip sets.

Remove 3 squares from the left end of 2 strip sets.

9. Measure the pieced center medallion from edge to edge through the center. Adjust the 4 short strips (17 squares each) to that measurement by increasing or decreasing seam allowance widths between the squares as needed. Sew the adjusted strips together in pairs to make 2 checkerboard border strips. Sew strips to opposite sides of the center medallion. Press the seams toward the center medallion.

10. Repeat step 9, adjusting and sewing the remaining checkerboard border strips to the center medallion. Press the seams toward the center medallion.

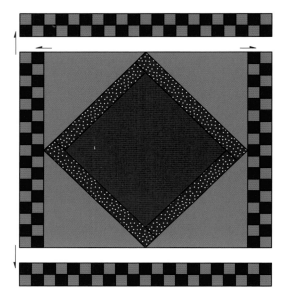

11. Measure the center medallion as described in step 9 and cut 2 outer border strips for the center medallion from the 2"-wide orange strips. Sew the strips to the center medallion and press the seams toward the outer border strips. Repeat to add the remaining orange border strips. Set completed center medallion aside.

ADDING THE APPLIQUÉS

1. Refer to "Adding Appliqués" on page 16 to prepare the appliqués. Use the appliqué template patterns on pages 76–77 for the moon, trees, frog, and dragonflies.

2. Referring to the photograph on page 53 and the illustration below for placement, position the appliqués and fuse them in place in numerical order.

3. If desired, machine buttonhole stitch over the edges of each appliqué shape.

PIECING THE CRAZY BLOCKS

1. Arrange the 10" squares in 5 decks of 10 each (you will have 2 extra squares). Each deck should contain 10 different prints. Secure each deck with a pin through all layers until ready to sew.

2. Referring to "Making the Crazy Blocks" on page 9, make 50 five-segment whole blocks. Trim the blocks to 8" x 8".

Assembling the Quilt Top

1. Arrange the side setting triangles and blocks in diagonal rows, with the center medallion in the middle. Arrange the blocks, moving and turning them, until you are satisfied with the arrangement. Try to arrange the blocks so that identical prints are not side by side in the finished layout.

2. Referring to the quilt assembly diagram, sew the rows together in the units shown and press as directed by the arrows; then add the units to the center medallion in numerical order. Add the corner setting triangles last.

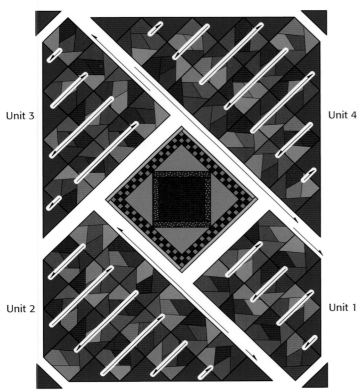

Quilt Assembly

3. Sew the strips for the inner border together to make 1 long strip. Trim to size and sew to the quilt as directed in "Adding the Borders" on page 16. Press the seams toward the inner border strips. Repeat with the strips for the outer border. Press the seams toward the outer border strips.

4. Add appliqués to the lower left corner of the quilt top. Embellish with buttonhole stitching if desired.

Finishing Your Quilt

1. Divide the backing fabric crosswise into 2 panels, each approximately 94" long. Remove the selvages and join the pieces along 2 long edges to make the backing. Press the seam to one side.

2. Layer the quilt top with batting and backing with the backing seam parallel to the long edges of the quilt top. Baste the layers together with your favorite method (see page 18).

3. Hand or machine quilt as desired.

4. Trim the backing and batting even with the quilt-top edges and bind the quilt (see page 20).

5. Add a label to the back and enjoy your new quilt.

In the Boy's Room

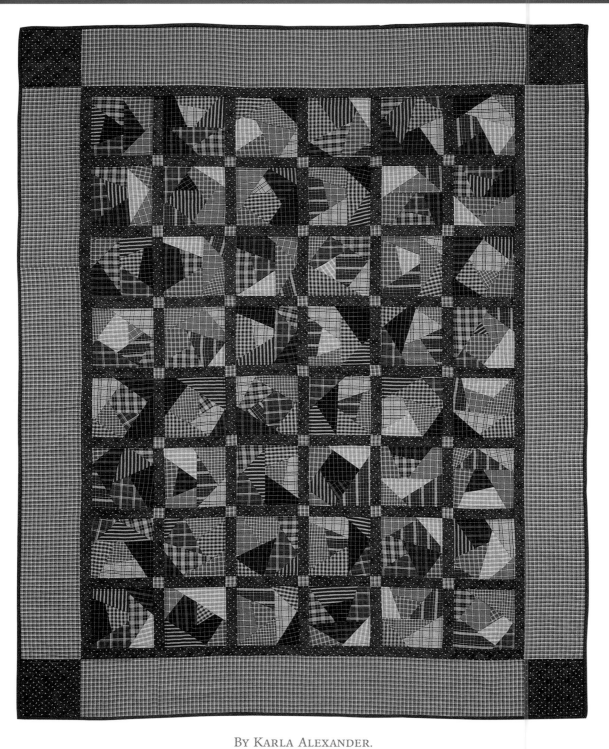

BY KARLA ALEXANDER.
PIECED BY JOANNA PRICE AND QUILTED BY SARAH STOWELL.
Finally there's a quilt that really works in a boy's room! Inspired by fond memories of my older
brothers Terry and Bruce in their plaid shirts, I designed this easy-to-make quilt. The resulting rustic look is very "boyish."

Sizes and Block Requirements

Finished Size: 62" x 78"

Finished Crazy Block Size: 6¾" x 6¾"

Crazy Block Requirements: 48 Seven-Segment Whole Blocks

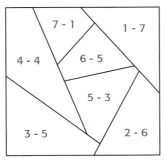

Block Sewing and Cutting Guide
Cut Size: 10" x 10"

MATERIALS

Yardage is based on 42"-wide fabric, with 40" of usable width after preshrinking.

⅜ yd. *each* of 12 different plaid prints for Crazy blocks

1⅜ yds. dark print for sashing, inner border, and outer border corner squares

1⅔ yds. plaid for cornerstones and outer border

⅝ yd. dark print for binding

4¾ yds. fabric for backing

66" x 82" piece of batting

CUTTING

All measurements include ¼"-wide seam allowances.
Cut all strips across the fabric width (crosswise grain).

From *each* of the 12 plaid prints for Crazy blocks, cut:

1 strip, 10" wide, for a total of 12 strips; crosscut each strip into 4 squares, 10" x 10", for a total of 48 squares.

From the dark print for sashing and borders, cut:

1 strip, 6" wide; crosscut strip into 4 squares, each 6" x 6", for outer border corner squares.

17 strips, each 1¾" wide; crosscut strips into a total of 82 strips, each 1¾" x 7¼", for sashing.

6 strips, each 1¾" wide, for inner border

From the plaid for cornerstones and outer border, cut:

7 strips, each 6" wide, for outer border

2 strips, each 1¾" wide; crosscut strips into 35 squares, each 1¾" x 1¾", for cornerstones

From the dark print for binding, cut:

8 strips, each 2½" wide

PIECING THE CRAZY BLOCKS AND SASHING STRIPS

1. Arrange the 10" squares into 6 decks of 8 each. Each deck should contain 8 different plaid prints. Secure each deck with a pin through all layers until ready to sew.

2. Referring to "Making the Crazy Blocks" on page 9, make 48 seven-segment whole blocks. Trim the blocks to 7¼" x 7¼".

3. Use 5 cornerstones, each 1¾" x 1¾", and 6 sashing strips, each 1¾" x 7¼", to make 1 horizontal sashing strip. Repeat to make 7 sashing strips. Press all seams toward the sashing strips.

Make 7 sashing strips.

ASSEMBLING THE QUILT TOP

1. Arrange the blocks into 8 horizontal rows of 6 blocks each, with a 1¾" x 7¼" sashing strip between each pair of blocks. Play with the blocks, moving and turning them until you are satisfied with the arrangement.

2. Pin and sew the sashing strips and blocks together in rows. Press the seams toward the sashing strips. Number the block rows for reference when sewing them together to make the quilt top.

Make 8 block rows.

3. Sew a long horizontal sashing strip to the lower edge of block rows 1–7. Press the seams toward the sashing strips.

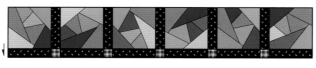

Make 7.

4. Sew the sashed block rows together in numerical order. Press the seams toward the sashing.

5. Sew the 1½"-wide strips for the inner border together to make 1 long strip. Press the seams open. Repeat with the 6"-wide strips for the outer border.

6. Trim the inner border strips to size and sew them to the quilt top as directed in "Adding the Borders" on page 16. Press the seams toward the border strips.

7. Measure the quilt-top width through the center as you did for the inner border. Cut 2 outer border strips to this measurement from the long strip sewn in step 5. Sew a 6" outer border corner square to each short end of the strips. Press the seam toward the corner square. Set aside.

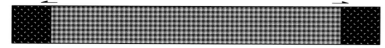

Make 2.

8. Measure the quilt-top length through the center as you did for the inner border. Cut 2 outer border strips to this measurement from the remaining strip sewn together in step 5. Sew strips to the quilt-top side edges. Press the seams toward the inner border.

9. Sew the top and bottom outer border strips with corner squares to the quilt top. Press the seams toward the inner border.

FINISHING YOUR QUILT

1. Divide the backing fabric crosswise into 2 equal panels, each approximately 84" long. Remove the selvages and sew the pieces together along 2 long edges to make the backing. Press the seam to one side.

2. Layer the quilt top with batting and backing, with the backing seam parallel to the short edges of the quilt top. Baste the layers together with your favorite method (see page 18).

3. Hand or machine quilt as desired.

4. Trim the backing and batting even with the quilt-top edges and bind the quilt (see page 20).

5. Add a label to the back and enjoy your new quilt.

BY KARLA ALEXANDER

Precious memories of evenings with my friend Lindy Lee were the inspiration for this cuddly flannel quilt.

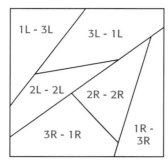

Block Sewing and Cutting Guide
Cut Size: 11" x 11"

MATERIALS

Yardage is based on 42"-wide fabric, with 40" of usable width after preshrinking.

⅜ yd. *each* of 12 different flannel prints for Crazy
    blocks*

⅓ yd. fabric for inner border

1¼ yds. fabric for outer border

3½ yds. fabric for backing

⅝ yd. fabric for binding

59" x 75" piece of batting

*Choose your favorite colors. I selected a soft color palette of dusty blues and lavenders in a variety of shades.

CUTTING

All measurements include ¼" seam allowances. Cut all strips across the fabric width (crosswise grain).

From *each* of the 12 flannel prints for Crazy blocks, cut:

   1 strip, 11" wide, for a total of 12 strips.
      Crosscut each strip into 3 squares, 11" x 11",
      for a total of 36 squares.

From the inner border fabric, cut:

   6 strips, each 1½" wide

From the outer border fabric, cut:

   7 strips, each 6" wide

From the binding fabric, cut:

   7 strips, each 2½" wide

PIECING THE CRAZY BLOCKS

1. Arrange the 11" squares in 4 decks of 9 squares each. Each deck should contain 9 different prints. Secure each deck with a pin through all layers until ready to sew.

2. Referring to "Making the Crazy Blocks" on page 9, make 36 six-segment two-sided blocks. Trim the blocks to 9" x 9". You will have an extra block that will not be used in the project.

ASSEMBLING THE QUILT TOP

1. Arrange the blocks into 7 rows of 5 blocks each. Move and turn the blocks until you are satisfied with the arrangement. Try to arrange the blocks so that identical prints are not side by side in the finished quilt layout.

2. Pin and sew the blocks together in horizontal rows. Press the seams in alternating directions from row to row.

3. Sew the rows together and press the seams in one direction.

4. Sew the strips for the inner border together to make 1 long strip. Press the seams open. Repeat with the strips for the outer border.

5. Trim to size and sew the inner border strips to the quilt top, following the directions in "Adding the Borders" on page 16. Press the seams toward the inner border strips.

6. Add the outer border in the same manner as the inner border.

FINISHING YOUR QUILT

1. Divide the backing fabric crosswise into 2 panels, each approximately 62" long. Remove the selvages and join the pieces along 2 long edges to make the backing. Press the seam to one side.

2. Layer the quilt top with batting and backing with the backing seam parallel to the top and bottom edges of the quilt top. Baste the layers together with your favorite method (see page 18).

3. Hand or machine quilt as desired.

4. Trim the backing and batting even with the quilt-top edges and bind the quilt (see page 20).

5. Add a label to the back and enjoy your new quilt.

Festive Angel and Holly Table Runners

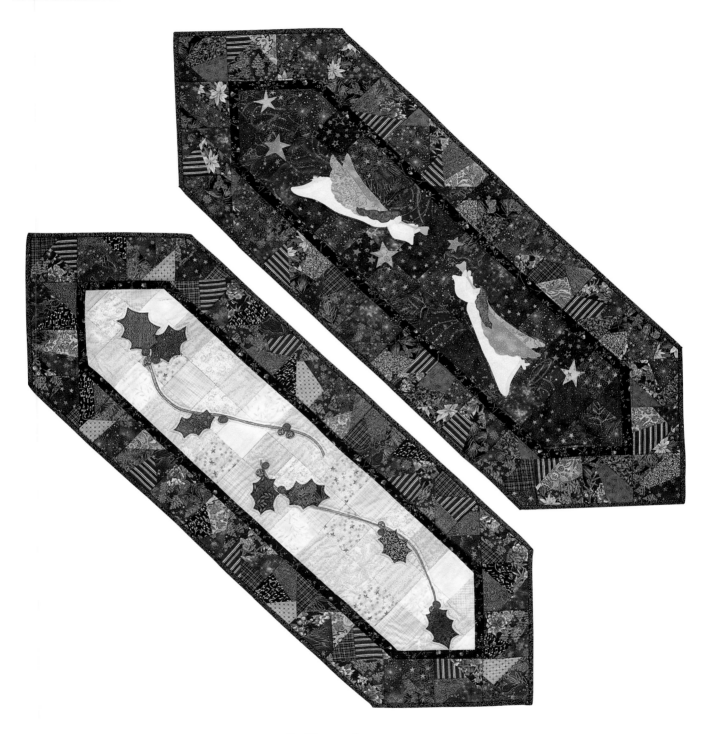

BY KARLA ALEXANDER

Crazy block borders surround pieced centers in each of these runners. The appliqué work is easy
with fusible web, and it is embellished with buttonhole and straight stitching at the outer edges.

Sizes and Block Requirements

Finished Size: 18½" x 56"

Finished Crazy Block Size: 4" x 4"

Crazy Block Requirements: 35 Four-Segment Whole Blocks

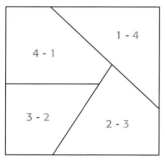

Block Sewing and Cutting Guide
Cut Size: 6½" x 6½"

Note: For help with fabric colors and placement, refer to project photos on page 63.

MATERIALS FOR ONE TABLE RUNNER

Yardage is based on 42"-wide fabric, with 40" of usable width after preshrinking.

¼ yd. *each* of 9 assorted prints for patchwork center (runner center)

¼ yd. fabric for inner border

¼ yd. *each* of 6 different holiday prints for Crazy blocks

1 yd. fabric for backing

⅜ yd. fabric for binding

1½ yds. fusible web for appliqués

MATERIALS FOR ANGEL APPLIQUÉS

⅛ yd. skin tone fabric for face, hands, and feet

⅛ yd. brown for hair

⅛ yd. white for dress

⅛ yd. gold for wings and stars

⅛ yd. golden brown for horns

MATERIALS FOR HOLLY APPLIQUÉS

Assorted green scraps for leaves

⅛ yd. brown for branches

Assorted red scraps for berries

CUTTING

All measurements include ¼"-wide seam allowances. Cut all strips across the fabric width (crosswise grain).

From *each* of the 9 assorted prints for the patchwork center, cut:

1 strip (9 total), 3½" x 20"

From any of the 9 assorted prints for the patchwork center, cut:

1 square, 4" x 4"; cut square once diagonally to yield 2 small triangles for points.

1 square, 5½" x 5½"; cut square twice diagonally to yield 4 large triangles for side points.

From *each* of 2 of the 9 assorted prints for the patchwork center, cut:

1 square (2 total), 3½" x 3½", for points

From the inner border fabric, cut:

3 strips, each 1½" wide

From *each* of the 6 holiday prints for Crazy blocks, cut:

1 strip, 6½" wide, for a total of 6 strips. Crosscut each strip into 6 squares, 6½" x 6½", for a total of 36 squares.

From the binding fabric, cut:

5 strips, each 2½" wide

PIECING THE PATCHWORK CENTER

1. Sew 2 large triangles to opposite sides of the 3½" squares for the points of the runner. Press the seams toward the triangles. Add a small triangle at the top of each square and press the seam toward the small triangle.

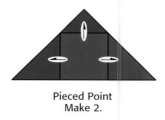

Pieced Point
Make 2.

2. Sew the nine 3½" x 20" strips together to make a strip set and press the seams in one direction. Crosscut the strip set into four 3½"-wide segments.

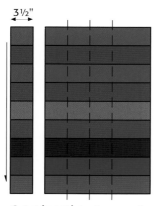

Cut strip set into 4 segments.

3. Sew two 3½"-wide segments together, short end to short end, to make a long strip with 18 squares. Repeat with the remaining 2 segments.

Make 2.

4. At the right end of one strip, remove the 6 end squares. Repeat at the left end of the remaining strip.

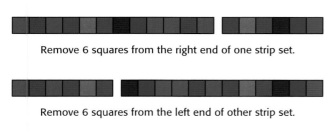

Remove 6 squares from the right end of one strip set.

Remove 6 squares from the left end of other strip set.

5. Sew the 6-square strips together to make 1 long strip of 12 squares.
6. Arrange the three 12-square strips as desired and sew them together to make the patchwork center. Press the seams in one direction.

Note: Before you sew the strips together, check to see that the seams are pressed in opposite directions from strip to strip. You may need to re-press the seam allowances in one or more strips.

7. Sew a pieced point made in step 1 to each short end of the patchwork center. Press the seams toward the patchwork center.

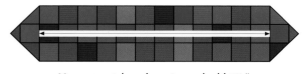

8. To add the inner border strip, measure patchwork center, beginning and ending at the joining seams for the points. Cut 2 inner border strips to match that measurement plus 1½" and sew 1 to each long edge of the patchwork center. Press the seams toward the border strips.

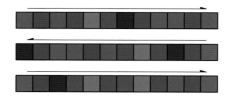

Measure patchwork center and add 1½".

9. Trim the ends at an angle, even with the edges of the points as shown.

Trim even with diagonal edges.

10. Measure the length of one edge of one of the points and add 2". Cut 4 inner border strips to this measurement. With the excess strip extending at the side edges of the patchwork center, pin and sew an inner border strip to each side of each point. Press the seams toward the border strips. Trim the excess strip even with the edges of the side inner border strips.

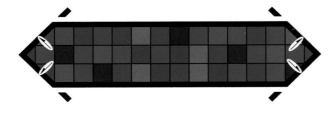

ADDING THE APPLIQUÉS

1. Using the appliqué template patterns on pages 78–79 for the angels or the holly, prepare the appliqués as directed in "Adding Appliqués" on page 16.

2. Referring to the photographs on page 63 and the illustrations below for placement, position the appliqués and fuse them in place in numerical order. For the angel, it's easiest to position the larger pieces first and then tuck the smaller pieces in under the edges as needed before fusing everything in place.

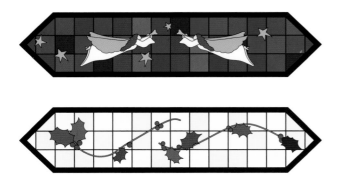

3. Buttonhole or straight stitch around appliqué shapes for a finished look.

PIECING THE CRAZY BLOCKS

1. Arrange the 6½" squares into 6 decks of 6 squares each. Each deck should contain 6 different prints. Secure each deck with a pin through all layers until ready to sew.

2. Referring to "Making the Crazy Blocks" on page 9, make 36 four-segment whole blocks. Trim the blocks to 4½" x 4½". You will have an extra block that will not be used in the project.

ASSEMBLING THE TABLE RUNNER

1. Place the pieced and appliquéd table runner on a large, flat surface. Arrange the Crazy blocks around the outer edges, with 10 blocks along each long edge and 7 blocks surrounding each pointed end.

2. Sew the Crazy blocks together in the desired order to make 2 strips of 10 blocks each for the sides. Center, pin, and sew 1 strip to each long edge of the runner. There should be excess fabric at each end of each long edge. Trim the excess even with the angle of the point, *saving the scraps for step 3.* Press the seams toward the inner border.

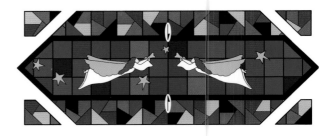

3. For each end of the runner, sew Crazy blocks together to create a 4-block strip and a 3-block strip. Sew a scrap from step 2 to one end of each strip as shown.

Make 2.   Make 2.

4. Sew a 3-block strip to one side of each point. Press the seams toward the inner border. Trim excess even with the edges of the runner. Repeat with the 4-block strips.

FINISHING YOUR TABLE RUNNER

1. Divide the backing fabric lengthwise into 2 panels, each approximately 36" long. Remove the selvages and join the pieces, short end to short end, to make the backing. Press the seam open.
2. Layer the table runner with batting and backing, centering the table runner on the strip with the backing seam perpendicular to the long edges of the runner. Baste the layers together with your favorite method (see page 18).
3. Hand or machine quilt as desired.
4. Trim the backing and batting even with the pieced table runner and bind the edges (see page 20).
5. Add a label to the back and enjoy your table runner.

Festive Tree Skirt

By Karla Alexander.

Quilted by Sally Blankenship.

Here's a great way to use all of your favorite holiday prints—a Crazy block Christmas tree skirt.
This project also makes a great table topper if you prefer—just don't cut out the inner circle.

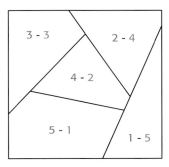

Block Sewing and Cutting Guide
Cut Size: 11" x 11"

MATERIALS

Yardage is based on 42"-wide fabric, with 40" of usable width after preshrinking.

⅜ yd. *each* of 12 Christmas prints for Crazy
blocks

2¼ yds. fabric for backing

1 yd. fabric for binding

1 yd. strong string or cord

Chalk pencil

CUTTING

*All measurements include ¼"-wide seam allowances.
Cut all strips across the fabric width (crosswise grain).*

**From *each* of the 12 Christmas prints for Crazy
blocks, cut:**

  1 strip, 11" wide, for a total of 12 strips.
    Crosscut each strip into 3 squares, 11" x 11",
    for a total of 36 squares.

From the binding fabric, cut:

  Enough 2½"-wide bias strips to make a 370"-
    long piece

PIECING THE CRAZY BLOCKS

1. Arrange the 11" squares in 3 decks of 12 each. Each deck should contain 12 different prints. Secure each deck with a pin through all layers until ready to sew.

2. Referring to "Making the Crazy Blocks" on page 9, make 36 five-segment whole blocks. Trim the blocks to 9" x 9".

ASSEMBLING THE TREE SKIRT

1. Arrange the blocks in 6 rows of 6 blocks each. Play with the blocks, moving and turning them until you are satisfied with the arrangement. Try to arrange the blocks so identical prints are not side by side in the finished layout.

2. Pin and sew the horizontal rows together. Press seams in opposite directions from row to row. Sew the rows together and press the seams in one direction.

FINISHING THE TREE SKIRT

1. Cut two 13"-wide strips from the backing fabric, cutting across the fabric width. Sew the strips together at the short ends and press the seam open (see illustration in step 2 on page 70).

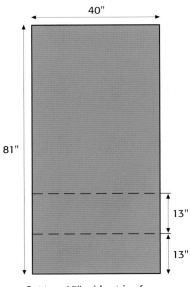

Cut two 13"-wide strips from
the end of backing fabric.

2. Sew the strip to 1 long edge of the remaining piece of backing and press the seam open. Trim the excess as shown.

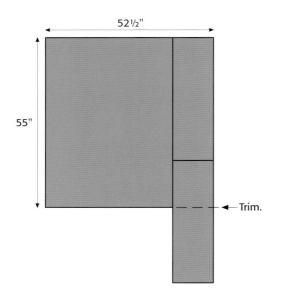

3. Layer the backing with the batting and the patchwork on top. Baste the layers together with your favorite method (see page 18).
4. Hand or machine quilt as desired.
5. Place the quilted patchwork face up on a large carpeted or padded surface, and anchor it with a straight or T-pin at the center of the patchwork. Tie a 30"-long piece of strong string or cord to the pin and tie the other end of the string to a chalk pencil so the resulting string is 25" long. Draw a circle, using the string and chalk as your compass. Shorten the string to 3" from pin to chalk and mark a 6"-diameter center circle for the tree-trunk opening. Draw a straight line from the inner circle to the outer circle. Cut on the marked lines.

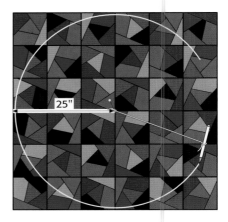

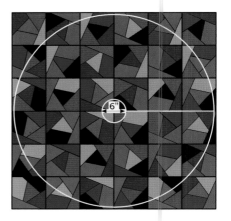

6. Sew the bias strips together to make 1 long piece of binding and bind all raw edges of the tree skirt as directed in "Binding Your Quilt" on page 20.
7. Add a label to the back and enjoy your tree skirt.

Velvet Pillow

By Karla Alexander

Using machine embroidery stitches is the perfect way to quilt and embellish the Crazy blocks in this plush pillow.

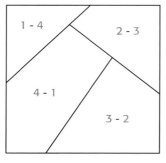

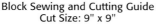

Block Sewing and Cutting Guide
Cut Size: 9" x 9"

MATERIALS

All measurements include ¼"-wide seam allowances.

9 different 9" squares of velvet for Crazy blocks

17" square of velvet for pillow back

18" square of batting

PIECING THE CRAZY BLOCKS

1. Stack the 9" squares.
2. Referring to "Making the Crazy Blocks" on page 9, make 9 four-segment whole blocks. Trim the blocks to 6" x 6".

ASSEMBLING THE PILLOW

1. Arrange 3 rows of 3 blocks each. Move and turn the blocks until you are satisfied with the arrangement.
2. Sew the blocks together in rows and finger-press the seams open. Sew the rows together and finger-press the seams open.
3. Place the pillow top face up on the batting and use spray basting (see page 18) to hold the layers together.
4. Machine quilt as desired. Consider embellishing the seams with decorative stitching instead of a straight line of quilting.
5. Follow the finishing instructions for the pillow on page 28 to complete your velvet pillow.

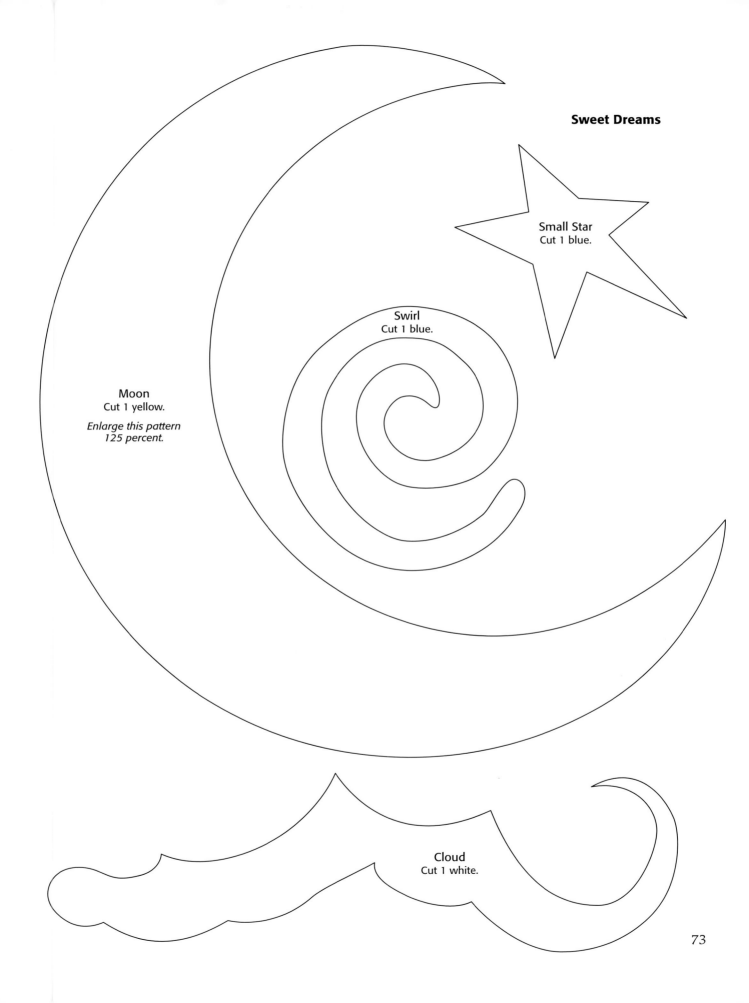

Sweet Dreams

Small Star
Cut 1 blue.

Swirl
Cut 1 blue.

Moon
Cut 1 yellow.

*Enlarge this pattern
125 percent.*

Cloud
Cut 1 white.

73

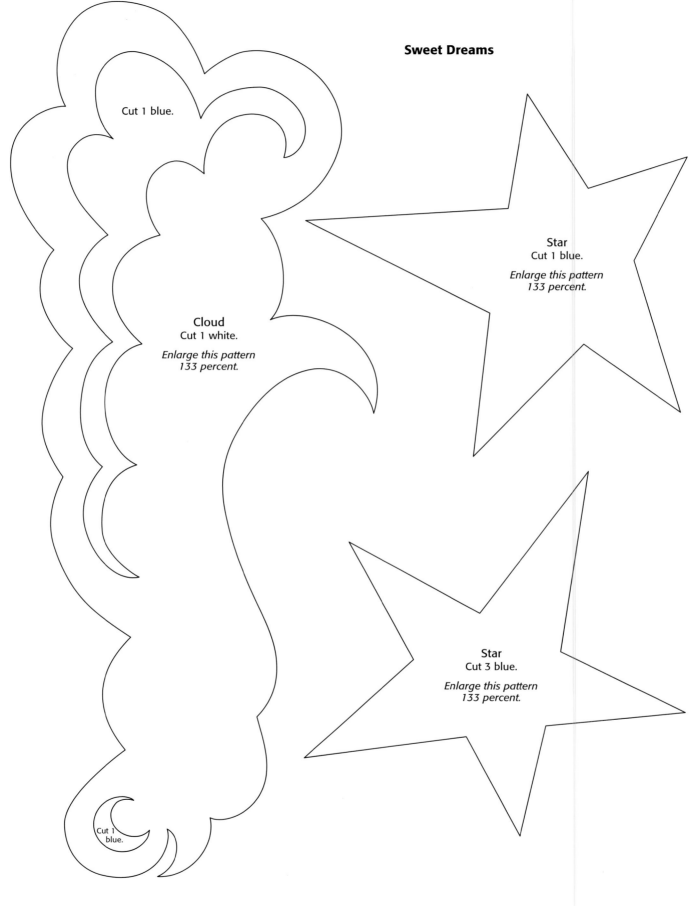

Sweet Dreams

Cut 1 blue.

Cloud
Cut 1 white.

*Enlarge this pattern
133 percent.*

Star
Cut 1 blue.

*Enlarge this pattern
133 percent.*

Star
Cut 3 blue.

*Enlarge this pattern
133 percent.*

Cut 1
blue.

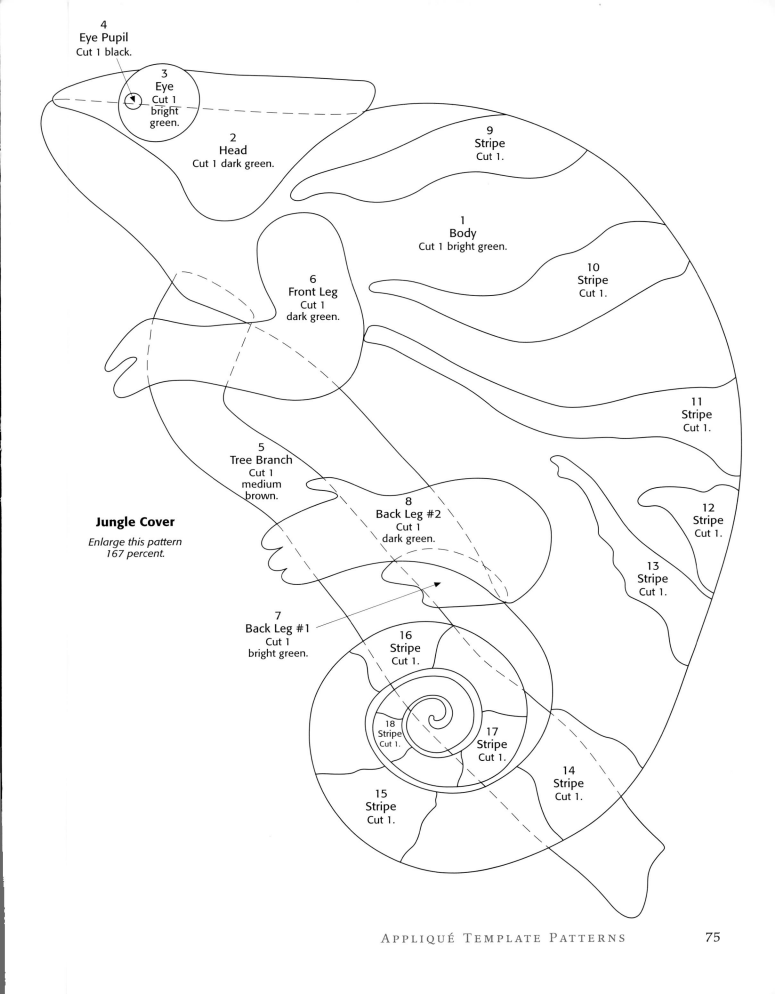

4
Eye Pupil
Cut 1 black.

3
Eye
Cut 1
bright
green.

2
Head
Cut 1 dark green.

9
Stripe
Cut 1.

1
Body
Cut 1 bright green.

6
Front Leg
Cut 1
dark green.

10
Stripe
Cut 1.

11
Stripe
Cut 1.

5
Tree Branch
Cut 1
medium
brown.

8
Back Leg #2
Cut 1
dark green.

12
Stripe
Cut 1.

Jungle Cover

*Enlarge this pattern
167 percent.*

13
Stripe
Cut 1.

7
Back Leg #1
Cut 1
bright green.

16
Stripe
Cut 1.

14
Stripe
Cut 1.

18
Stripe
Cut 1.

17
Stripe
Cut 1.

15
Stripe
Cut 1.

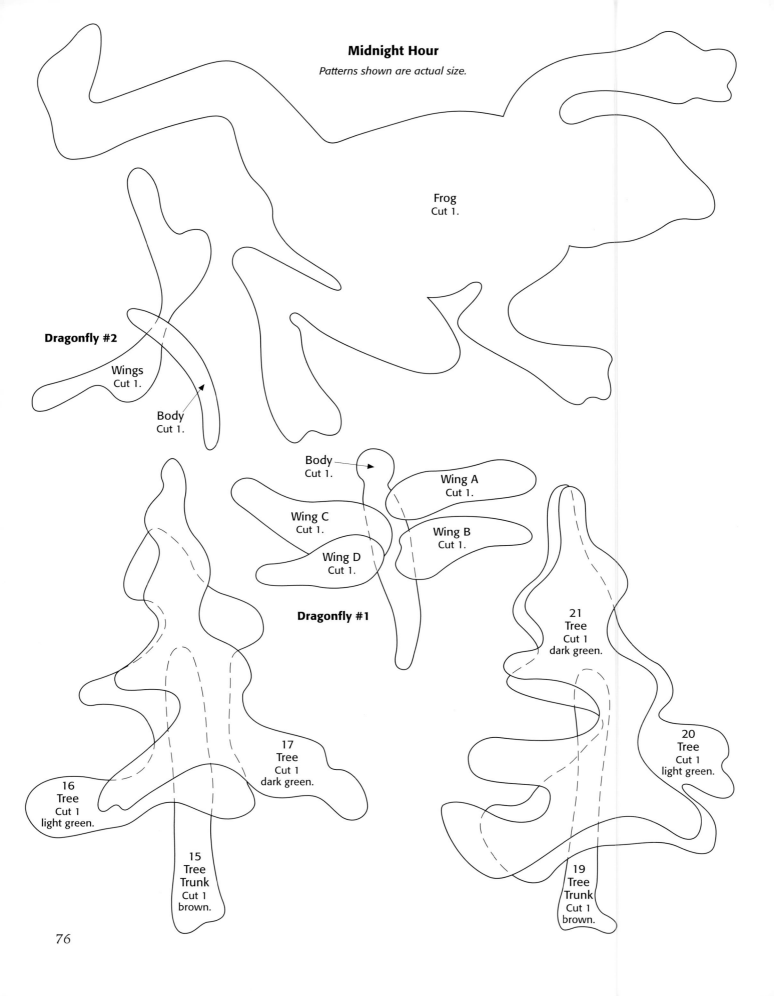

Midnight Hour

Patterns shown are actual size.

Frog
Cut 1.

Dragonfly #2

Wings
Cut 1.

Body
Cut 1.

Body
Cut 1.

Wing A
Cut 1.

Wing C
Cut 1.

Wing B
Cut 1.

Wing D
Cut 1.

Dragonfly #1

21
Tree
Cut 1
dark green.

17
Tree
Cut 1
dark green.

16
Tree
Cut 1
light green.

20
Tree
Cut 1
light green.

15
Tree
Trunk
Cut 1
brown.

19
Tree
Trunk
Cut 1
brown.

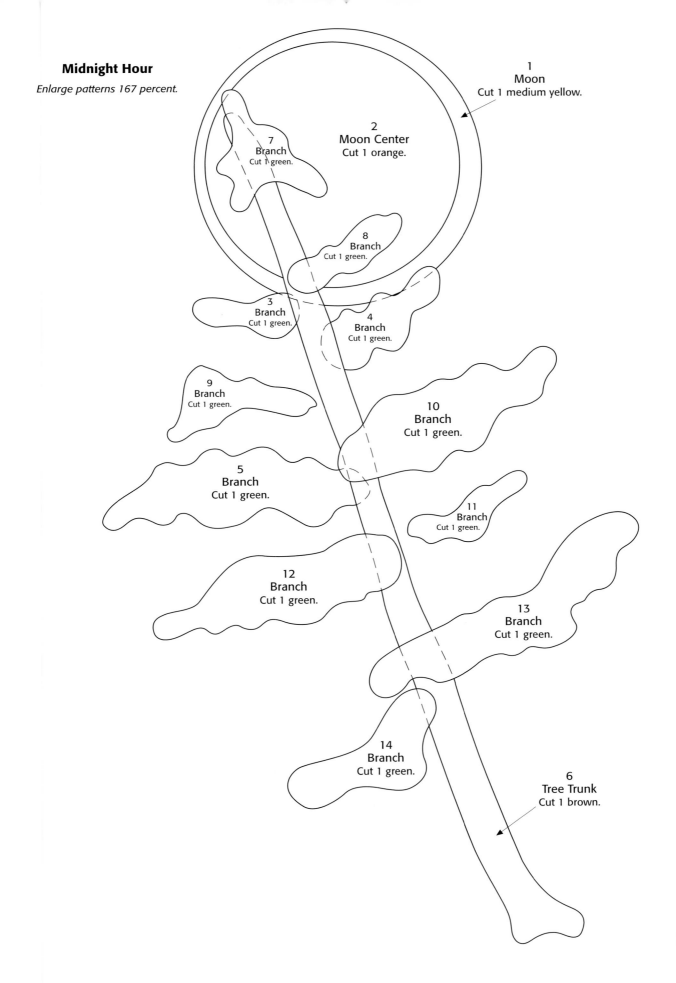

Midnight Hour

Enlarge patterns 167 percent.

1
Moon
Cut 1 medium yellow.

2
Moon Center
Cut 1 orange.

7
Branch
Cut 1 green.

8
Branch
Cut 1 green.

3
Branch
Cut 1 green.

4
Branch
Cut 1 green.

9
Branch
Cut 1 green.

10
Branch
Cut 1 green.

5
Branch
Cut 1 green.

11
Branch
Cut 1 green.

12
Branch
Cut 1 green.

13
Branch
Cut 1 green.

14
Branch
Cut 1 green.

6
Tree Trunk
Cut 1 brown.

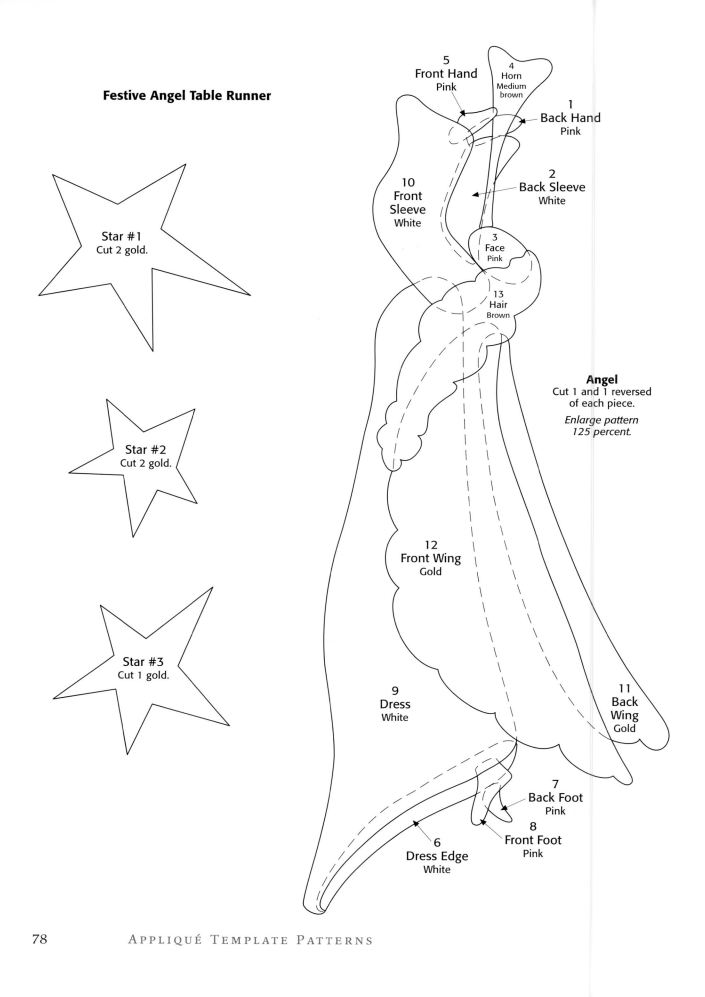

Festive Angel Table Runner

Star #1
Cut 2 gold.

Star #2
Cut 2 gold.

Star #3
Cut 1 gold.

5
Front Hand
Pink

4
Horn
Medium
brown

1
Back Hand
Pink

2
Back Sleeve
White

10
Front
Sleeve
White

3
Face
Pink

13
Hair
Brown

Angel
Cut 1 and 1 reversed
of each piece.

*Enlarge pattern
125 percent.*

12
Front Wing
Gold

9
Dress
White

11
Back
Wing
Gold

7
Back Foot
Pink

8
Front Foot
Pink

6
Dress Edge
White

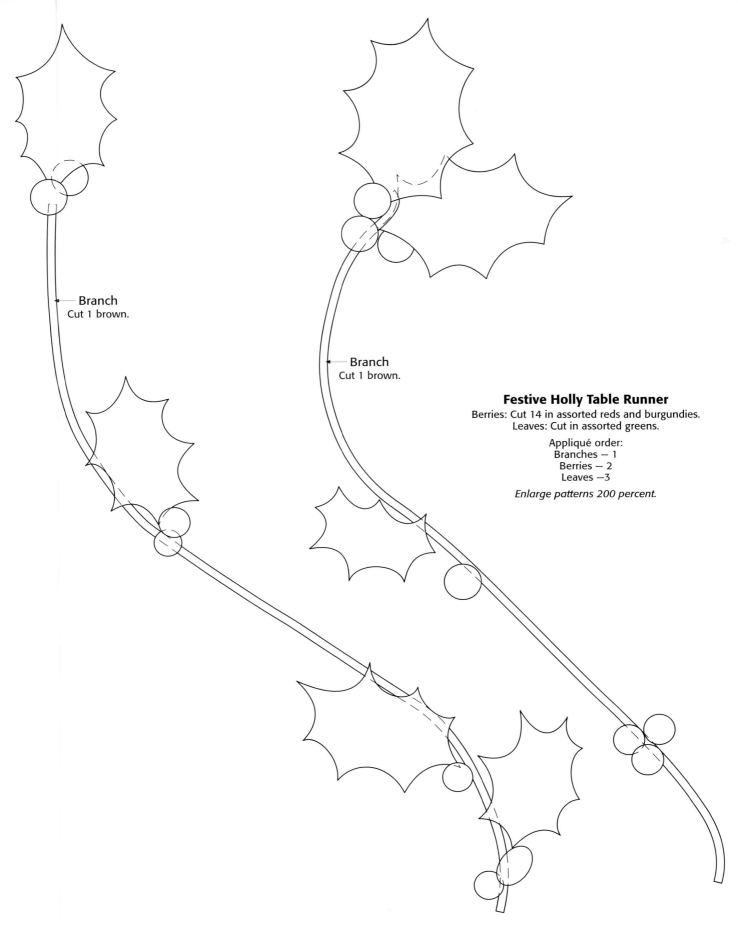

Branch
Cut 1 brown.

Branch
Cut 1 brown.

Festive Holly Table Runner
Berries: Cut 14 in assorted reds and burgundies.
Leaves: Cut in assorted greens.

Appliqué order:
Branches — 1
Berries — 2
Leaves —3

Enlarge patterns 200 percent.

 As a young girl, Karla Alexander enjoyed pinning and arranging fabric scraps together, the beginning of her lifelong love of creating quilts. As a teenager, the gift of a quilt sparked her appreciation of the art of quilt-making. Years later, while living in Kodiak, Alaska, Karla faced the challenge of dark, rainy winters and long summer days by exploring quiltmaking. Today, her pastime has grown into a passion for the endless possibilities of quilts.

Since 1997, Karla has taught quilt classes and designed and written patterns. A featured teacher at many quilt retreats, she has taught over four thousand students and made well over one hundred quilts. Karla now lives in beautiful Salem, Oregon, with her husband, Don, and youngest son, William. Her oldest son, Shane, lives in Idaho, and her second son, Kelly, is enlisted in the navy. Karla currently teaches and works at Greenbaum's Quilted Forest in Salem and takes great pleasure in inspiring quiltmakers of all ages and skill levels.